ISLANDICA

A SERIES RELATING TO ICELAND AND THE
FISKE ICELANDIC COLLECTION
CORNELL UNIVERSITY LIBRARIES

EDITED BY VILHJÁLMUR BJARNAR

VOLUME XLI

HALLDÓR HERMANNSSON
By P. M. Mitchell

Halldór Hermannsson

Halldór Hermannsson in the Fiske Icelandic Collection, 1946

Halldór Hermannsson

BY

P. M. MITCHELL

ISLANDICA XLI

CORNELL UNIVERSITY PRESS

Ithaca and London, 1978

First published 1978 by Cornell University Press.
Published in the United Kingdom by Cornell University Press Ltd.,
2-4 Brook Street, London W1Y 1AA.

International Standard Book Number 0-8014-1085-1
Library of Congress Catalog Card Number 77-14665
Printed in the United States of America by Vail-Ballou Press, Inc.
Librarians: Library of Congress cataloging information
appears on the last page of the book.

Preface

Halldór Hermannsson was curator of the Fiske Icelandic Collection at Cornell University from 1905 to 1948. Between 1908 and 1958 he wrote or compiled thirty-two volumes of the series *Islandica*. This present volume, which commemorates the centenary of his birth on 6 January 1878, is an attempt to review his life as a scholar and to abstract his published works.

Since the Fiske Icelandic Collection is to such a large extent the work of Halldór Hermannsson, it provided the essential font of information for the compilation of this centenary memorial. I am grateful to Vilhjálmur Bjarnar, curator of the collection, for advice and unstinting assistance. To the Cornell University Libraries I should like to take this opportunity to express my appreciation for having been allowed to make use of the collection for more than four decades.

For encouragement and help I thank Finnbogi Guðmundsson, Ólafur F. Hjartar, and Ólafur Pálmason of the National Library of Iceland, where I completed a revision of the bibliography originally compiled by Stefán Einarsson. Earlier, much searching and checking were done at the Library of the University of Illinois and the Royal Library in Copenhagen.

P. M. M.

Urbana, Illinois

Contents

Illustrations

Halldór Hermannsson

I

From "Íþaka" to Ithaca

While the history of Halldór Hermannsson's career may seem explicable only by an appeal to the element of chance, there is a common denominator at every stage in his life: the love of books and the pursuit of knowledge. Adjudged from either a linear or a metaphysical standpoint, the progress from a rural farm in Iceland to Cornell University in Ithaca, New York, by way of Denmark and Italy, is radical, but Halldór's bibliophilia and learning can explain this movement and minimize the distances and apparent contrasts involved. His familiarity with books and his bibliothecal predilection together with a dedication to learning must have been the characteristics that originally recommended the twenty-one-year-old Icelander to the former professor of North European languages and librarian at Cornell University, Willard Fiske, in 1899, the year which in retrospect seems to have been crucial in Halldór's life.

All evidence indicates that Halldór Hermannsson acquired his love of books early. He had grown up in a home with a good library, and when he went to the Latin school—"Hinn lærði skóli" ("The learned school")—in Reykjavik, he was immediately attracted to the library and came to function there as a volunteer worker with the responsibility of lending books to the other pupils in the school. It is a

Halldór Hermannsson (*back row, second from right*) in secondary school, Reykjavik, ca. 1896

curious and seemingly prophetic coincidence that the book collection of the Latin school in Reykjavik was named Íþaka—that is, "Ithaca." The name had been chosen as a gesture to Willard Fiske, who, during his sojourn in Iceland in 1879, inspired the establishment of a new reading society at the school and who subsequently was a benefactor of the society.

Halldór, who had been born at Völlur, in the Rangárvellir district of Iceland on 6 January 1878, was sent to Reykjavik to attend the Latin school there in 1892; he finished his schooling and passed the university matriculation examination on 30 June 1898 as the salutatorian of his class of seventeen.

Even before completing his secondary education in Iceland, Halldór had begun writing for the Icelandic newspaper *Ísland.* He produced résumés of Danish and Norwegian articles and books about conditions in various parts of the world—and in so doing demonstrated at this early date his catholic interest in current events the world over. All the articles from the years 1897 to 1899 were printed pseudonymously or anonymously, and although Halldór mentioned at times that he had written for "the papers" in his student days, it has not previously been determined which articles stemmed from his pen. All the articles written prior to his departure for Copenhagen in the summer of 1898 were signed by a pseudonym: either Hrærekur, Heiðrek(u)r, or Hjeðinn. Since the editor of *Ísland*, Þorsteinn Gíslason, later stated in an article about Halldór in the illustrated monthly *Óðinn* in 1909, that Halldór had contributed articles about foreign affairs to *Ísland*, the pseudonymous articles signed by names all beginning with "H" might well be assumed to be contributions by Halldór Hermannsson. When one discovers, however, that all the pseudonyms, which were taken

Halldór Hermannsson (*seated*) at his graduation from secondary school in Reykjavik, 1898

from saga literature, are the names of persons whose patronymics or cognomens also begin with "H," the circumstantial evidence seems indisputable. The pseudonymous articles ceased when Halldór went to Denmark; instead there appeared a series of letters containing news from abroad ("Frá útlöndum"), all dated from Copenhagen between 25 September 1898 and April 1899, that is, prior to his taking his first comprehensive examination at the university of Copenhagen and then leaving for Italy.

He was not to write extensively for the ephemeral press in Iceland again except in the years 1909 and 1910, when he contributed a series of articles bearing new pseudonyms ("Peregrinus" and "Sig. Lontano," both of which suggested his peregrinations and Italian experience) to Þorsteinn Gíslason's weekly paper *Lögrjetta*.

As was the wont of young Icelanders seeking higher education prior to the founding of the University of Iceland, Halldór went to Copenhagen after graduating from secondary school. He matriculated at the University of Copenhagen in the College of Law, where he was nominally enrolled until 1904. In starting the study of law, he was following a family tradition: his father had been a district judge (*sýslumaður*) and his two brothers also studied law. Like most other serious students, he took the preliminary examination that granted the interim degree of *candidatus philosophiæ* after a year of study, in 1899. That summer he was introduced to Willard Fiske. Fiske had come to Copenhagen from Florence, Italy, where he had been living since 1883, in order to acquire more Scandinavian books and to seek one or two young Icelanders who could assist him in organizing the very large collection of Icelandic books and periodicals he had assembled in the preceding years.[1] Two law students,

[1] The interested reader is referred to Horatio S. White's *Biography of Willard Fiske*, published by the Oxford University Press in 1925; to the

Bjarni Jónsson and Halldór Hermannsson, subsequently accompained Willard Fiske to Florence and started work on the collection. Bjarni Jónsson returned to Copenhagen after a year in Florence, while Halldór worked for Willard Fiske, although not continuously, until Fiske's death in 1904.

Willard Fiske had started collecting Icelandic books when he was a student in Sweden in the early 1850's, but it was not until he had become an expatriate that he could vigorously and systematically pursue his interest as a collector of not only Icelandic books but items in Rhaeto-Romanic, and books on Petrarch, Dante, and runology as well. During his trip to Iceland in 1879 he had, to be sure, acquired many Icelandic books and established associations with Icelandic men of letters and booksellers which enabled him to collect more efficiently in succeeding years and to track down older Icelandic books of which only a few copies existed. After 1883, however, he was in constant communication with booksellers in the search for Icelandic works that interested him. He bid at many auctions. In the preface to volume I of the *Catalogue* of the Fiske Icelandic Collection, Halldór reports that, according to his own estimate, Fiske acquired some 800–900 volumes and 3,000 pamphlets during the summer of 1899 alone. Halldór quotes Fiske's words in expressing an intent to secure all publications that "throw light on the history, topography, indigenous products, commerce, language, and letters of Iceland." Perhaps because Fiske had (as Halldór explains in the same preface) never kept a record of his purchases and had preserved only some of the bills he

---

"Memorial to Willard Fiske" constituting vol. XII, nos. 3–4, of *The Papers of the Bibliographical Society of America*, Chicago, 1918; and to three volumes of short works by Willard Fiske, which were published as *Memorials of Willard Fiske* in Boston, 1920–22. For a spirited description of Fiske's ambivalent relationship to Cornell University, see Morris Bishop's *History of Cornell*, Ithaca, 1962, pp. 224ff.

had paid, subsequently making it difficult to trace the development of the collection or to determine the provenience of any given book, Halldór himself was careful to preserve all business letters and bills as the collection grew under his supervision in the New World.

We have little detailed information about Halldór Hermannsson's activities between 1899 and 1904. Most of the time he spent in Florence, Italy, working for Willard Fiske. He made several trips between Florence and Copenhagen in those years. Between June and November of 1904 he was employed by the Royal Library in Copenhagen. Here he worked in the map and picture division of the library—a fact which probably contributed to the lasting concern with cartography evidenced in several of the volumes of *Islandica*.

When Willard Fiske died in 1904, he left most of his books and considerable capital to Cornell University. In his testament, which among other things established the Icelandic Collection and determined that it should have a curator born and educated in Iceland, Fiske suggested that Halldór Hermannsson be appointed to the curatorship. He established a fund from which the salary of the curator should be paid; a second fund, the revenues from which should purchase books for the Icelandic Collection; and a third to support the publication of an annual volume about Iceland or the Icelandic Collection. For the first few years after 1904, possibly even up to World War I, these funds were adequate to fulfill the needs for which they were established, but in time they grew less than adequate and eventually quite inadequate, so that they had to be supplemented to fulfill Fiske's intentions.

The meeting with Fiske was something of a meeting of minds, for the two men shared several interests, above all in books and chess. Halldór, who called chess "the queen of games," played chess with Fiske in Florence, and the two of them published in 1901 and 1902 a periodical in Icelandic on chess, *Í uppnámi*. Halldór was, however, the sole editor of the second volume, 1902. Although Reykjavik was the nominal place of publication, the periodical was printed in Leipzig.

Willard Fiske had assembled a great deal of material on chess and other games in Iceland; this interest was reflected in his posthumously published book that Halldór saw through the press: *Chess in Iceland and in Icelandic Literature with Historical Notes on Other Table-Games*. The book appeared in Florence in 1905 with the imprint of "The Florentine Typographical Society," which was but a way of saying the book was published privately by the executors of Willard Fiske's estate. Most of the book has the running head "stray notes," a phrase that fairly well characterizes its contents, for in essence the book is not a history of chess in Iceland, nor does it develop a single argument. Were it not for the index at the back of the book, it would be difficult to use profitably. This index is in part the work of Halldór Hermannsson, as we know from a remark by Horatio S. White in the preface; but which parts of the book derived from Halldór's assistance to Fiske and how much discussions between Fiske and his Icelandic amanuensis helped form the ideas and factual information Fiske put into writing are matters of conjecture. Fiske had examined the proofs of all but the last twenty pages of text and had even compiled a portion of the index before his death (in Frankfurt am Main) on 17 September 1904. He had also begun to write a preface that spoke of plans to issue a second volume on various matters pertaining to chess in Iceland, but the subject was not pursued after Fiske's death.

Fiske had compiled a series of *Bibliographical Notices* that were issued privately in five numbers in Florence between

1886 and 1890. Numbers I, IV, and V lists books printed in Iceland between 1578 and 1844 as supplements to the catalogue of the British Museum. Fiske had started to compile a fourth listing of additional Icelandic items as the sixth small volume in the series. The bibliographical supplement was completed by Halldór Hermannsson and published in 1907 in Ithaca, albeit with no indication of a publisher, which must be assumed to have been Cornell University Library.

In volume XII of *The Papers of the Bibliographical Society of America*, 1918 (which comprised the "Memorial to Willard Fiske"), there is an article by Halldór on Fiske and Icelandic bibliography in which he assesses the Icelandic Collection briefly and speaks of Fiske's own contributions. He describes Fiske as "one of the most agreeable men to work with I have known," "painstaking in everything to which he devoted himself . . . quick in understanding things and in discerning the important and essential points when dealing with books" (p. 106). These traits made Fiske a compatible employer and fellow scholar; they were also traits Halldór himself shared. On an important point they differed: Halldór did not have Fiske's failing of starting "on something new before he had completed what he had been working on" (ibid.).

During the first two decades of the century, when the funds left by Willard Fiske had sufficed or nearly sufficed to keep up with the ever-increasing production of the presses of Iceland, the Icelandic Collection grew at a rapid rate. In 1927, Halldór published the second catalogue of the collection, which recorded additions made to the collection between 1913 and 1926. Almost all of these additions had been published since 1912, although a very few older books had been acquired. Unlike the first volume of the catalogue, the second records many volumes of foreign fiction in

Icelandic translation. Music and books about music, which had scarcely been represented in volume I, were now more abundant. In the preface to volume II Halldór notes the increase in scholarly publications in Iceland since the establishment of the University of Iceland in 1911. He also points out that the political independence of Iceland granted in 1918 accounted for a large number of government publications issued in Iceland, as well as many reports, statistical, meteorological, and medical in nature, which previously would have been issued in Copenhagen. The number of newspapers and journals had multiplied, and most of these found their way to the collection in Ithaca. In 1914, when Halldór was in Iceland, he had acquired many separately printed occasional poems for the Collection, not because of their intrinsic value, but rather because, as he says, they represent "a curious custom, and are therefore well worth preserving." He adds with a bit of irony that such poems showed "how natural it is for the Icelanders to break out into verse on the slightest provocation" (p. vi). Curiously enough, unlike the majority of his countrymen, Halldór Hermannsson apparently never wrote any poetry.

The meeting with Fiske was decisive in determining the course of the young Icelander's life, for he and Fiske's Icelandic Collection gradually became inextricable. What was intended as a temporary job became a life work. When the Icelandic Collection traversed the Atlantic, Halldór Hermannsson followed it to that Ithaca "where Greek meets Indian," a small town surrounded by dairy farms and orchards—and to that institution at which a wealthy American idealist and freethinker had hoped "any person could find instruction in any subject"—Cornell University. The law of academic supply and demand did not work in Halldór's favor; he was really in a unique position in the United States that left him no choice: because of the Icelandic Collection he was bound to Cornell University. The alternative was to return to Scandinavia—from which feelers were sent out several times between 1920 and 1936.

As early as 1922 the Danish Ministry of Education had asked Bogi Th. Melsteð to try to convince Halldór to become head of the Arnamagnaean Collection of Icelandic manuscripts. Halldór was not uninterested in the proposition, as is known from a telegram of 22 December 1922 in which he indicated his willingness to accept the position if it were well enough paid. Nothing seems to have come of these maneuvers, however. The following March Bogi Th. Melsteð tried to promote the idea that Halldór be Valtýr Guðmundsson's successor as professor at the University of Copenhagen—but no concrete proposal seems to have been forthcoming in this connection. A return became a real possibility in 1925, when Halldór went to Copenhagen for a year as the curator of the Arnamagnaean Collection, with the view of occupying that position permanently. As a matter of fact, when the Copenhagen newspapers of the day reported his arrival and identified him as the new head of the Arnamagnaean Collection, they gave no indication that the appointment was a temporary one. Halldór had taken leave from Cornell University for a year, however, and therefore continued to have two options. At what juncture or for what reasons he decided to return to Cornell is unclear, but the decision seems to have been made after relatively few months in Copenhagen and perhaps in part because of the presence of Finnur Jónsson, who seems to have been a thorn in Halldór's side during that academic year. In his necrology of Finnur Jónsson in the *Journal of English and Germanic Philology*, 1935, Halldór notes that Finnur used the Arnamagnaean Commission and the Royal Society of Northern Antiquaries "virtually as his private publishers; all works issued under their auspices for a period of fifteen years had him as author

Halldór Hermannsson as a young man in Copenhagen

or editor. This was an unfortunate state of affairs, not only because some of the editions thus issued were not needed and were often prepared with the smallest amount of effort, but also because he thus prevented these institutions from adopting any definite plan, or policy, of publication in answer to modern needs . . ." (p. 475). The reasons for Halldór's decision probably were multiple, however, and were in part no doubt of a financial nature. But it may also be safely presumed that Halldór felt there was a commitment to be discharged toward the Fiske Icelandic Collection and the will of its founder, that there was much unfinished work in the collection that he was best able to perform, and that, after twenty years in Ithaca, the pattern of his own scholarly existence was well established.

Although the possibility of returning to Copenhagen or even Reykjavik was suggested again from time to time in the years to come, Halldór continued on the path that now was set until his retirement, first as professor, in 1946, and then as curator, in 1948. At the close of his career, Halldór Hermannsson, Willard Fiske's erstwhile helper of a half-century before, had purchased half again as many volumes for the Icelandic Collection as had Fiske himself, and had published an impressive series of studies for which the collection was the point of origin.

Halldór's attention was not fixed solely upon Iceland or Denmark, but in the New World he interested himself in every aspect of Icelandic culture that evoked a reflex here, as is evidenced by many articles pertaining to Icelanders in America and by his contributions in Icelandic publications issued on the North American continent. A characteristic article by Halldór Hermannsson was "Icelandic-American Periodicals" contained in the *Publications of the Society for the Advancement of Scandinavian Study* in 1916. Although many of the periodicals about which he was writing were partisan in one way or another, Halldór's attitude toward them was objective and factual. He records with satisfaction the continued affection of Icelanders on the North American continent for their mother country and their active interest in its affairs. He shared this affection and interest. The last sentence in his essay is anticipatory and optimistic: "Easier means of communication and mutual visits have cleared the air on both sides, and from the interchange of ideas both have benefited."

At the request of the Danish-Icelandic Society (Dansk-islandsk Samfund) Halldór Hermannsson wrote a forty-three-page pamphlet in Danish, *Islændere i Amerika*, in 1922. It comprises, first, a carefully researched history of the Icelandic settlements in North America including the names of many of the persons involved, the numbers of the settlers, and the names of the settlements. Second, it describes the role of churches among Icelanders in the New World and the activities of their congregations. The information Halldór assembled had been gleaned from a perusal of Icelandic-American newspapers and other periodicals. Third, the pamphlet describes the history of publishing in Icelandic, both in Canada and the United States, with special reference to belles-lettres, and here again pays special attention to the acknowledged greatest Icelandic-American—or Icelandic-Canadian—poet, Stephan G. Stephansson. Giving an example of a well-known Icelandic-American, Halldór described succinctly the life and early work and writings of Vilhjalmur Stefansson, the Arctic explorer.

While Halldór expressed admiration for much that had been written in Icelandic in the New World and for the efforts made to keep the Icelandic cultural heritage alive, he believed that the loss of the Icelandic language among second- or third-generation Icelanders in North America was inevitable. He spoke with pride of the character and achievements of Icelandic immigrants. They had, he wrote, done honor to the country of their birth and given it a good name in their new surroundings. Halldór Hermannsson, one may note, did the same.

II

Keys to Scholarship

Once established in Ithaca, Halldór Hermannsson had as his initial tasks bringing the Icelandic Collection into some systematic order and making it accessible to scholarship so that it could be exploited productively. To this end he set out to prepare the manuscript of an alphabetical catalogue of the collection's holdings with the intent of having the catalogue printed as soon as possible. The first catalogue of the Icelandic Collection was not a mere enumeration of items taken from the card file of the collection which had been worked out while it was housed outside Florence. Indeed, the implications of the preparation of such a catalogue and its ramifications are scarcely evident to anyone who has not been engaged in a similar undertaking. Since Halldór was involved with a growing collection that, when brought to the United States, had comprised some 8,000 volumes, and which on the completion of volume I (1914) of the catalogue of the collection comprised some 10,200 volumes, merely the magnitude of the task is impressive. Nevertheless, the catalogue was completed in a relatively short time and without any secretarial assistance whatsoever.

Halldór found that the entries in the preliminary and partial card catalogue prepared in Florence were too brief. He was forced to review all the material and devise a means of recording and describing the books which represented a compromise between the ideal catalogue that Willard Fiske had envisaged and the extant card catalogue. Halldór explains that it had been Fiske's intention to publish a catalogue, but that the instructions he gave to this end were so detailed that the catalogue Fiske envisaged could scarcely have come into being. With its indices, volume I of the catalogue as prepared by Halldór Hermannsson comprises over 750 pages; Halldór estimated that a catalogue completed according to Fiske's instructions would have been six or seven times as large. A method of listing, adequate for scholars yet simple and practical, was needed, and decisions had to be made regarding how much information to include and how to arrange the material. Title pages had to be transcribed conscientiously and according to rules established for the endeavor. Pagination and the existence of plates also had to be recorded, and not infrequently some observations about the content of the item and its relation to other publications were desirable. Since the collection was intrinsically Icelandic, greater care was given to books written in Icelandic than in other languages. Icelandic titles were ordinarily given in full, at least through the year 1850, with an indication of abbreviations and the use of archaic characters (printed in italics). Only in the case of older non-Icelandic books preserved in the collection were titles given so precisely and completely. In preparing the catalogue of the collection, Halldór was confronted with a problem regarding the alphabetization of Icelandic names. Since most Icelanders had patronymics, rather than family names, and since the Icelandic custom is to alphabetize according to first name rather than patronymic, Halldór's decision to list writers by their patronymics or family names was arbitrary—but one for which there was widespread precedent. Some reviewers (and notably Paul Herrmann, writing in the *Deutsche*

Literaturzeitung for 1914), although complimentary about the catalogue itself, objected to the failure to follow Icelandic usage. Since the Icelandic system was then used only by Icelanders, and the catalogue was published for scholars the world over, however, Halldór's decision seems justifiable and in accord with the international usage that has obtained until very recently, when the Library of Congress decided to list modern Icelandic authors by their given names rather than their patronymics. Following certain bibliothecal examples, Halldór had disregarded the umlaut in ä, ö, and ü, but had put the Icelandic letter þ (thorn) at the end of the alphabet when, as Sigfús Blöndal pointed out, one might have expected it under English *th*. While Sigfús, reviewing the catalogue in *Nordisk Tidskrift för Bok-och Biblioteksväsen* II (1915), 178–82, wanted more cross-references in the catalogue, he praised Halldór for providing original titles for translations where the original title was not apparent. Several reviewers expressed their gratitude for the comprehensive index appended to the catalogue, which makes it easy to locate material on any given theme pertaining to Iceland. In his cheerful and enthusiastic fashion, Sigfús Blöndal wrote (p. 182) that while Iceland never would be able to thank Fiske adequately for his life work and the foundation of the collection that bears his name—one could at least thank Halldór Hermannsson for gaining international recognition for the collection and making it useful.

Realizing that biographical information on many of the authors represented was hard to come by, Halldór added the dates of authors in the catalogue in many cases. As Stefán Einarsson pointed out in 1958, this meant that the catalogue served as a biographical as well as a bibliographical reference work for many years prior to the publication of the standard biographical works on Icelanders which came into being some decades later.

The supplement to the catalogue published in 1927 takes account of the addition of some 6,000–7,000 items to the collection. When the compilation of the second supplement to the catalogue was completed in 1942, the collection comprised 21,830 items. That is to say, some 5,000 items had been added between 1927 and 1942, despite the fact that the monies available for buying books had diminished in purchasing power. The principles upon which the two supplements were worked out were the same as those for the first volume, although a few corrections of listings in the original catalogue and the first supplement are included in the second. Both supplements are also provided with subject indices, although by 1942 Halldór Hermannsson began to doubt that the use of such indices justified the time and labor involved in producing them.

In his preface to the second supplement to the catalogue (1943), Halldór points to the vigorous tradition of imaginative literature in Iceland, and in particular to the increase in the number of juvenile books written both by natives and foreigners which were appearing in Icelandic. He also mentions an increase in the number of translations into Icelandic, especially from the English, but speaks critically of the apparently haphazard way in which works of contemporary literature were selected for translation. He devotes a paragraph to the Icelandic scientific works that had increased noticeably in number in the foregoing twenty-five years, and expresses special satisfaction with the new series of scholarly editions of older Icelandic literatures such as *Íslenzk fornrit*. The collection came clearly to reflect the currents of publishing in Icelandic through Halldór's unflagging attention to Icelandic conditions and his tenacity in acquiring all significant and representative books, pamphlets, periodicals, and newspapers to augment the all-embracing collection Willard Fiske had begun.

In Willard Fiske's Icelandic Collection were found some 500 items that pertain to runology and that had for the most part only a tenuous connection with Iceland. The decision was therefore made to compile a separate catalogue of the runological items. Although Halldór had the manuscript of the catalogue ready by the spring of 1915, the book itself was not issued until 1918. The delay was caused by World War I, for the book was printed in England and published by Oxford University Press as *Catalogue of Runic Literature Forming a Part of the Icelandic Collection Bequeathed by Willard Fiske*.

There was, to be sure, a slight overlap with the previously issued catalogue of the Icelandic Collection. Consequently, items that had been included in the Icelandic Collection proper are identified by an asterisk in the *Catalogue of Runic Literature*. In addition to books and pamphlets, the runic material assembled by Fiske includes some coins, which are photographically reproduced on a plate included in the *Catalogue of Runic Literature*, and a wooden runic calendar dated 1661. In a short preface, Halldór gives a brief summary of the history of runes and runology. As with the catalogue of the Icelandic Collection, he provides a detailed subject index. He also includes an index of reviewers and other persons named in the notes to the books listed.

While some small replicas of runestones that Fiske had acquired in Copenhagen were preserved in the Icelandic Collection, Halldór did not direct his energies to problems of runology again except when he was asked to give his opinion on the so-called Kensington stone, which he could adjudge as fraudulent from a philological standpoint.

In his will, Willard Fiske had bequeathed $5,000 to the University, the income from which should be used to publish an annual volume relating to Iceland and the Icelandic Collection. According to Cornell University Librarian George W. Harris' preface to the first volume of *Islandica*, as the series came to be entitled, Fiske had suggested that the annual volume might "contain an accession list of the Collection, or papers, etc., on, *e.g.*, the discovery of America by the Norsemen." The volumes constituting *Islandica* have on the whole realized these suggestions made by Fiske. Although the curator of the Icelandic Collection was nowhere charged with compiling the volumes of the annual himself, Halldór undertook to produce the first numbers in the series, and the obligation that he continue apparently grew of itself, so that Halldór Hermannsson came to write the first thirty-one volumes of *Islandica*.

After evaluating the general situation in Icelandic studies and bearing Fiske's admonition in mind, Halldór, in consultation with George W. Harris (nominally the editor of the new series), decided that the preparation of several bibliographies were primary scholarly desiderata. As is well known in the world of libraries, *Islandica*, together with the three volumes of the printed catalogue of the collection published in 1914, 1927, 1943, constitutes the corpus of Icelandic bibliography. Of the forty volumes which have appeared in the series, sixteen are bibliographical—either enumerative and critical bibliography or bibliographical essays. Three of the first five volumes of *Islandica* contain enumerative bibliographies of the sagas; volume XIII, published in 1920, is a bibliography of the *Eddas*. Volume I, entitled *Bibliography of the Icelandic Sagas and Minor Tales*, published in 1908, is devoted to the so-called *Íslendinga sögur* written (with a few exceptions) before the end of the fourteenth century. The bibliography records all editions in the original Old Norse–Icelandic, all translations, and the critical literature issued before 1908 dealing with the *Íslendinga sögur*, as well as reviews of books listed. Each saga is identified briefly with some remarks about its origins and probable provenance. While the bulk of the material recorded is to be found in the Fiske Collection, Halldór

Hermannsson included those few items of which he knew that are not in the collection, in order to make the bibliography as nearly exhaustive as possible. Any bibliography of such nature eventually needs to be supplemented, and addenda to several of the early bibliographies were eventually published. A supplement to the first bibliography, on the *Íslendinga sögur*, was issued in 1935 as *Islandica* XXIV, and was, as Halldór mentions in his preface, almost as large as the original bibliography. Incidentally, the supplement contains an index of authors, editors, illustrators, and reviewers mentioned in both volumes I and XXIV of *Islandica*. As Halldór acknowledges, it had been easier for him to compile the supplement than the original bibliography since several periodical bibliographies pertaining to Scandinavian history and literature were now appearing in various journals. In the preface, he defends his own earlier bibliographies against the criticism of being too inclusive by listing out-of-date and unimportant studies. He observes, "I do not consider this a blemish. It is the bibliographer's task to record everything without distinguishing between whether it is good or bad, old or new. A work that seems now to be of no value may often be illustrative of the study and interpretation of the literature in question in times gone by." This principle continued to guide bibliographies appearing in the series *Islandica*.

From its first volume on, the series *Islandica* called forth numerous reviews. In the bibliography of Halldór Hermannsson's works appended here, one can find seventeen reviews and bibliographical acknowledgments of volume I of *Islandica* alone. The reviews evidenced considerable enthusiasm in academe for the new series. It was apparent that a very useful tool was being issued by a meticulous scholar through the offices of Cornell University. The series immediately assumed the character of a standard work. Bernhard Kahle, writing in the *Deutsche Literaturzeitung*

XXIX (1908), col. 3150, calls the first volume "ein ungemein wertvolles bibliographisches Hilfsmittel." Kahle was particularly impressed by Halldór Hermannsson's ability to locate items in periodicals that were not readily accessible.

While volume II of *Islandica* is a bibliography on the Norsemen in North America (to be discussed in Chapter V) and volume IV a bibliography of ancient laws (discussed below), volumes III and V make up with volume I a bibliography of the Old Norse–Icelandic sagas. Volume III, published in 1910, is the *Bibliography of the Sagas of the Kings of Norway and Related Sagas and Tales* while volume V (1912) is the *Bibliography of the Mythical-Heroic Sagas*, that is, the so-called "Fornaldarsögur" or sagas of ancient times. In the three volumes the individual sagas or short stories (*þættir*) are listed alphabetically and extant manuscripts are recorded, frequently with critical remarks regarding the age and origin of the saga or the manuscript, sometimes including observations about the interrelationship of various versions or recensions. There follows a listing of all the printings of a saga or *þáttr* in the original, whether separately or in a collection. Following this are recorded all known translations of the work. Finally, in lesser type, is found the critical literature about the work, including reviews. The length of individual entries naturally varies. The most comprehensive entry is for Snorri Sturluson's *Heimskringla;* the saga with the lengthiest entry is *Njáls saga*.

Unlike the two earlier bibliographies, the one covering the mythical-heroic sagas begins with a brief section that lists collections of texts in the original and in translation plus general critical-historical works dealing primarily with heroic saga and legends. Each of the volumes contains an appendix: volume I, of imaginative literature based on the Icelandic sagas (an area Halldór expressed a desire to deal with more thoroughly in the future, although this wish was never realized); volume III, of certain other works related to the sagas of the kings; and volume V, on Saxo Grammaticus, the sixteenth-century chronicle of Hven, and three spurious sagas.

The compilation of the three bibliographies could scarcely have been made so quickly were it not for the comprehensive nature of Willard Fiske's Icelandic Collection; while limited in scope, the collection was nearly exhaustive in coverage. There was, however, considerable research and footwork involved, in addition to a sifting of the material found in books and periodicals within the collection.

Halldór's study of law at the University of Copenhagen was not obliterated by his later studies. It is reflected in his publication of the bibliography of ancient laws of Norway and Iceland, which constitutes volume IV of *Islandica*, issued in 1911, as well as in his familiarity with legal documents on which he often drew in preparing commentaries on texts he edited. The compilation of the bibliography of early laws was not really a direct outgrowth of Halldór's work in the Fiske Collection, since so many of the titles recorded were not preserved there.

Halldór asks the reader to observe how little attention Scandinavian law has attracted in the English-speaking world and expresses the hope that more attention will be given to the subject in the future. A corollary of this hope is the existence of his bibliography, which for the first time identifies in a compact and summary way both primary and secondary material pertaining to ancient Scandinavian law. In a review of the bibliography in *Deutsche Literaturzeitung* XXXII (1911), cols. 2953–54, Professor Karl Lehmann of the University of Göttingen mentions several additional items that might have been included in the Bibliography but remarks astutely, "Das Wort vom leichter tadeln, als besser machen trifft auf sie besonders zu [The saying that it is easier to find fault with something than to improve it is especially applicable to such a work.]," for Halldór Hermannsson was here making an original bibliographical thrust.

With respect to scholarship dealing with early modern times, Halldór's most welcome and useful bibliographical contributions are *Islandica* IX and *Islandica* XIV, which describe the Icelandic books of the sixteenth and seventeenth centuries respectively. Both volumes are annotated bibliographies of the known works from those two centuries, with extensive comments about the individual books and mention of critical work done on them. Volume IX, *Icelandic Books of the Sixteenth Century* (1916), is augmented with several plates and line drawings.

Willard Fiske had compiled a tentative list of the Icelandic books of the sixteenth century in the late 1880's and had tried to ascertain where copies of those books were to be found. All such books were already scarce a century ago; they have become greater rarities and have appreciated in monetary value. Halldór based his own compilation on the notes Fiske had left, but Halldór personally examined all the sixteenth-century books that were found in the National Library in Reykjavik and in the Royal Library and University Library in Copenhagen. In all, forty-nine books, copies of which still exist, were recorded, in addition to a few other books that are known by title only.

In his introduction, Halldór sketches the history of printing through the end of the sixteenth century and discusses in particular the question whether there had been two active presses in Iceland in the last quarter ofthe sixteenth century; he comes to the conclusion that there must have been only one.

In *Icelandic Books of the Seventeenth Century* (*Islandica* XIV, 1922), 255 items are recorded, of which 134 had issued from the Hólar Press and 62 from the Skálholt Press in Iceland. Of the items enumerated, 28 are known by title only. Copies of most of the books are preserved in the Fiske Icelandic Collection, but Halldór had to travel to Reykjavik, Copenhagen, and London in order to be able to examine others and to describe them bibliographically in detail. One of the books, an edition of *Catonis Disticha* for Icelandic schoolboys, Halldór was to edit as volume XXXIX of *Islandica* twenty-six years later.

Like so many other of Halldór Hermannsson's works, the seventeenth-century bibliography was an exercise in perserverance and meticulousness. It was not a matter only of accurately describing books that were readily available, but also of tracking down books that were not enumerated in other works and of determining through circumstantial evidence the one-time existence of seventeenth-century books that had disappeared in intervening centuries. As in the bibliography of sixteenth-century books, Halldór recorded all books issued by the presses at Hólar and Skálholt, but also books by Icelanders printed outside of Iceland during the seventeenth century. Whereas the books in the sixteenth-century bibliography are listed chronologically, the seventeenth-century bibliography is alphabetical by author or by title so that various editions of the same work may be compared. Taken together, the two bibliographies, with the supplemental entries that were made in volume XXIX of *Islandica* in 1942, constitute an important segment of Icelandic national bibliography and have not been superseded. It is understandable that these two volumes of *Islandica* went out of print sooner than other volumes of the series.

Halldór's attention was not confined to earlier centuries. He also sensed bibliographical needs related to the contemporary situation and soon tried to fill a distressing lacuna:

in 1909, he circulated a printed form among Icelandic authors with the request for information about them and their publications. The answers he received became the basis of the biobibliographical compilation *Icelandic Authors of To-day*, volume VI of *Islandica* in 1913. Rather unexpectedly, the preface to this volume provides us with some of his views about his native land. He tries to answer the question put by foreigners who "on visiting Iceland have been astonished to find so much culture and literary interest in all classes of the population" and asked how this could be. Halldór believed that the explanation lay in the fact that "once having obtained a firm hold upon the mind of the people, the ancient Icelandic literature, in spite of many vicissitudes, never entirely lost its grasp" (p. vii). He then sketches briefly the history of Icelandic literature after the saga period, and speaks with approbation of the cultural nationalism that dates back to the end of the eighteenth century, despite the fact that the champions of the European Enlightenment (except the German thinker J. G. Herder and relatively few other influential minds) tended to lack understanding of "national traditions and their importance" (p. ix).

Halldór points out that there was renewed interest in Old Icelandic literature during the years of political unrest in Europe, in the first half of the nineteenth century. This he felt to be fortuitous circumstance, since the political alignment of those times implied a threat to the continued existence of the Icelandic language. Interest in the indigenous past developed the augmented national consciousness, which was of importance if the language was to continue to prosper. Perhaps for this reason, he grew kindly disposed to the popular doggerel-like verse called *rímur*, which until very recently has not enjoyed much prestige in Iceland. The importance of *rímur* and chapbooks for Icelandic literature

Halldór saw in their keeping an interest in narrative and song alive under unfavorable circumstances, as he put it the following year in the preface to his edition of *The Story of Griselda in Iceland* (*Islandica* VII, 1914).

He was gratified to observe that Icelandic literature, which was flourishing at the beginning of the twentieth century, helped assert the "independence both intellectually and politically" of the small nation (p. xi), although in point of fact Iceland did not regain its independence until 1918. Separating actuality from enthusiasm, he expressed satisfaction over the political autonomy won for Iceland in 1874 and extended in 1904. Despite his personal predilection for Copenhagen, Halldór shared the widespread Icelandic belief that the Danish governance of Iceland between the end of the fourteenth century and the end of the nineteenth century had meant maladministration and suppression. He had especially harsh words about the Danish commercial monopoly that "for two centuries paralyzed all enterprise, and stifled the initiative of the people" (p. xii). He concluded that because of the lack of initiative in practical affairs, Icelanders had turned to literary pursuits as a solace. He now welcomed the newly founded educational institutions in Iceland and said with pride that he doubted whether there was another group of men "of an equal number with so much fortitude and vitality as the Icelandic nation" (p. xii).

Icelandic Authors of To-day contains sketches of no fewer than 157 Icelandic writers in all disciplines—geologists, journalists and theologians, philologists, lawyers and botanists, as well as poets, dramatists, and narrators. The entries are after the manner of a who's who: place and date of birth, education, and vocation are accounted for, with mention of recognition or honors the person obtained. This is followed by a listing of published works—these lists are sometimes specific and detailed including contributions to periodicals, but sometimes brief and more general in nature. The discrepancy can probably be explained in most cases by the fullness or paucity of information furnished by the subject. The lengthiest entries are those of the philologists; other academics tend also to be rather explicit about their intellectual activities and publications. The longest single entry, three pages in small type, is on the scholar Finnur Jónsson, professor at the University of Copenhagen at the time—whose multifarious publications Halldór Hermannsson would speak critically of in a necrology in 1935. (See p. 23.) The shortest entry—two lines—is for the well-known poet Unnur Benediktsdóttir ("Hulda"), who, to be sure, was only in her thirties when the bibliography appeared.

In addition to works by any given author, translations the author made are also recorded, although oddly enough in most cases only by their Icelandic titles, and in some cases translations into foreign languages of the author's own works. Where such material had been published, biographies or biographical notices of the author were listed at the conclusion of the entry.

Striking is the number of writers—twenty-five—who were living and publishing in Canada in 1913. Five others had lived and written for a time either in Canada or the United States. Other expatriates were few; understandably, several Icelanders were living in Denmark, of which Iceland was still a legal—albeit autonomous—part.

Much of the information Halldór was able to assemble was otherwise difficult to come by, and some entries in the bibliography have remained principal sources of reference for information about the writers concerned.

Of more general interest than the earlier volumes of *Islandica* is the bibliographical essay *The Periodical Literature of Iceland down to the Year 1874* (*Islandica* XI), from the year

1918, which is an expository and critical discussion rather than an enumerative listing. It includes plates of the most important Icelandic publicists discussed and thirteen facsimiles of title pages.

In all, Halldór here reviewed no fewer than fifty Icelandic periodicals. In so doing, he was able to identify the social and political trends of nearly two hundred years. On page 95 he concluded that the process of regaining Icelandic independence in particular could be traced in the periodical literature: "First there came the movement for improving the economic conditions of the people by introducing liberty of trade and new methods and reforms in the principal forms of livelihood by the inhabitants. In the wake of this followed the efforts to elevate intellectual standards and literary taste, and finally the demand was made for self-government and political liberty." Specifically, Halldór looked upon the journal entitled *Ármann á Alþingi* (1829–32), written chiefly by Baldvin Einarsson, as revealing "the first awakening of the national spirit combined with a desire for increased knowledge and practical experience" (p. 40).

Many of the early Icelandic periodicals, although in the Icelandic language, were published in Copenhagen. Copenhagen was, after all, the center from which Iceland was governed, and it was at the University of Copenhagen that Icelanders studied until the early twentieth century. In this connection it will be recalled that Halldór himself followed the centuries-old pattern of the Icelander who sought higher learning by matriculating at the University of Copenhagen. An additional limiting factor was the existence of a single press (at Hólar except for a few years when it was at Skálholt) up to 1772. The following years a new press was set up at Hrappsey in the Skálholt diocese. Curiously enough, the first periodical to issue from the new press—a monthly newspaper—was in Danish, although it was edited by an Icelander.

Halldór had examined the contents of each of the periodicals he mentioned and described them in greater or lesser detail depending on the intrinsic importance of the journal and the impact it had. Up to 1773 periodical literature did not include reading material for the public but merely the annual reports of the Althing, starting with the year 1696. Periodical literature comparable with that in the countries of Western Europe dates only from 1781, with the establishment, in Copenhagen, of a series (*Rit*) of the first Icelandic Literature Society (Hið íslenzka Lærdómslistafélag, founded 1779). Halldór points out the variety of subjects treated in the fifteen volumes of the series which were published; included are even some notable translations, of which the most significant is Jón Þorláksson's Icelandic version of the first two books of Milton's *Paradise Lost.* Halldór has praise for the intent and work of the Society: "Many pages in its publications may still be read with pleasure and profit" (p. 15).

Of periodicals subsequently published, the longest lived is *Skírnir*, the first volume of which appeared in 1827 and which still is issued annually. Originally, Halldór points out, *Skírnir* superseded *Íslenzk sagnablöð* of the second Icelandic Literary Society (Hið íslenzka Bókmenntafélag, founded in 1816 as the successor to the earlier Lærdómslistafélag). To be sure, the nature of *Skírnir* has changed; it was originally a news annual, issued in Copenhagen. Place of publication was transferred to Reykjavik in 1890, and since 1905 it became a periodical "of miscellaneous contents"—to which Halldór himself contributed several times.

On pages 36–37, Halldór devotes some attention to the programs, or scholarly treatises, that were issued by the

Latin school at Bessastaðir, later Reykjavik, from 1828 through 1895. That the custom was then given up at a time when he himself was attending the Latin school, Halldór thought deplorable, since so many of the contributions had been of high quality. He calls particular attention to Sveinbjörn Egilson's prose translation of the *Odyssey*, which constituted six of the programs between 1829 and 1840, for he saw in this translation "the forerunner of the renaissance in the language and literature of Iceland" (p. 37). In a lengthy footnote on pages 37–38, Halldór records the authors and titles of all the programs, 1829–1895.

The actual renaissance of Icelandic literature Halldór attributes to the periodical *Fjölnir*; its nine volumes appeared in Copenhagen between 1835 and 1847, and were edited and written by several Icelandic students of whom the leader was Tómas Sæmundsson and the most agressive was Konráð Gíslason. Tómas Sæmundsson's introduction to the first volume Halldór characterizes as "a call such as the nation had never heard before" (p. 44). One of the major contributors to *Fjölnir* was Jónas Hallgrímsson; of the poems by Jónas printed in the journal's pages Halldór Hermannsson felt, "They set the standard by which poets were to be measured" (p. 47).

The successor to *Fjölnir* was the annual *Ný félagsrit*, 1841–73, which was chiefly the work of the Icelandic patriot Jón Sigurðsson, who dealt basically with political matters. "His articles were propaganda literature of the best kind," wrote Halldór Hermannsson; they were models of lucidity that "bear witness to his profound scholarship" (p. 61).

On the numerous other periodicals, almost all of them short lived, that were published from mid-century until the establishment of constitutional government in 1874—an ideal for which several of the journals agitated—Halldór passes brief qualitative judgment and provides the interested reader with biobibliographical footnotes for further information about particular journals and their editors. The only other serial publication to which Halldór accords notable intrinsic importance was the collection of older and newer documents augmented by critical commentary and issued as *Safn til sögu Íslands og íslenzkra bókmennta að fornu og nýju*, which started publication in 1853.

III

New Light on a Distant Island

When Halldór Hermannsson launched his scholarly career, foreign attention to Icelandic literature was, for historical and philological reasons, concentrated almost exclusively on the country's remarkable medieval heritage symbolized by the two words "Edda" and "saga." It was therefore natural that the first volume of *Islandica* should make contributions to the bibliography of Old Norse philology with special reference to the indigenous culture and achievements of Scandinavians, notably Icelanders. There remained, however, a large gray area in the history of Iceland of which foreigners with few exceptions—Willard Fiske was such an exception—had next to no knowledge or appreciation. It was consequently fitting that Halldór devoted several volumes of *Islandica* to cultural phenomena and important men of the postclassical era and, from a comparative standpoint, also tried to depict—nay, unveil—those literary associations with other countries that provided Icelandic writing with examples, prototypes, and motifs.

Halldór Hermannsson's edition of *The Story of Griselda in Iceland* (*Islandica* VII, 1914) is indicative of his efforts to delineate the role of Continental literature in Iceland—as is his edition of the *Physiologus* issued as volume XXVII of *Islandica* twenty-four years later. The existence of an Icelandic version of the Griselda story is in itself testimony both of a literary orientation toward the Continent and of the influx of popular foreign literature in Iceland—a phenomenon imperfectly explored and with implications yet to be determined fully. In point of fact, the Griselda volume realized a plan Willard Fiske had had thirty years previously and was an offshoot of Fiske's interest in Petrarch rather than of his Icelandic Collection. Fiske had gathered manuscript copies of several Icelandic versions of the Griselda story; Halldór's edition of the Griselda material was based on the copies Fiske had had made.

Halldór demonstrated that two of the Icelandic versions of the tale of Griselda were translations of a Danish chapbook first published in Copenhagen in 1597. Manuscripts of the earlier of these two Icelandic versions are to be found in the library of the British Museum and in the National Library of Iceland. The later version is preserved in manuscript in the Royal Library in Copenhagen. Halldór reproduced his text from the manuscript in the British Museum.

Although the story of Griselda was not printed in Iceland in the form of a chapbook, the various versions of the story which exist in Icelandic attest that it was well known and bespeak a widespread interest in the popular literature of adventure and sentimentality. In addition to the translations of the Danish chapbook, there are two versions of a saga of Gríshildur preserved in the National Library of Iceland. Halldór printed the text of the older of the two versions. There are, moreover, *rímur* that rework the Griselda story, written by a certain Eggert Jónsson in the seventeenth century. In his introduction to the volume, Halldór retells the story as contained in Eggert's version and quotes some of the stanzas. A seventeenth-century poem by Þorvaldur Rögnvaldsson composed some time after 1650 is printed in the section making up texts as the first of several versions of the Griselda story in Iceland. Halldór describes *rímur* reworking the Griselda story in 1778 and 1834, written by Páll Sveinsson and Magnús Jónsson respectively, as well as *rímur* on Griselda by Tómas Jónsson that were completed in January of 1801. These are not reproduced among the printed texts, however. Halldór explains that the several metrical versions of the Griselda story must be derived from a common source that differed from the prose renderings of the same story. Because of the evidence of certain names, he was inclined to think that the story came to Iceland from Holland and that the tradition probably was oral.

Halldór accounts for additional Icelandic versions of the Griselda story that are identified with a Duke Valtari and preserved in three manuscripts; Halldór printed the oldest of these (pp. 7–12), from the end of the seventeenth century, found in the Arnamagnaean Collection in Copenhagen. The younger manuscripts are an eighteenth-century version in the library of the British Museum and a nineteenth-century version in the National Library of Iceland. Halldór felt that internal evidence in the story of Valtari suggests something that had circulated orally, since the tale shows characteristics of oral storytelling in Iceland. He was inclined to believe that this version of the Griselda legend also may have come to Iceland through Germany or Holland.

Finally, Halldór reprinted the more recent, popular version of the legend as preserved in Jón Árnason's monumental nineteenth-century collection of Icelandic folk tales.

In his search for evidence about the condition and nature of the nonclassical literature of Iceland—that is, the literature produced between the Reformation and the nineteenth century—Halldór came upon a satire that originally had been written in Latin in 1703 and then rewritten in Icelandic about a decade later by its original author Þorleifur Halldórsson (1683–1713), whom Halldór depicts as having been among the most gifted Icelanders of his time. The original Latin version of the satire was entitled "Mendacii encomium"; the Icelandic version has no title, but was given an equivalent Icelandic title by Halldór: "Lof lýginnar," 'in praise of lying.' In 1915, as volume VIII of *Islandica* (*An Icelandic Satire*) Halldór edited the Icelandic text from a copy in the Bodleian Library at Oxford.

Although Þorleifur's work was not original in concept, it was, in Halldór Hermannsson's words, "noteworthy as the first indication in Icelandic literature of that realistic-rationalistic tendency, of that skeptical and inquiring spirit, which toward the end of the sixteenth century in Scandinavian countries began the struggle against dominant orthodoxy." The satire belongs to the general class of literature of which the best-known example is Erasmus' *Moriae encomium*. Instead of folly, Þorleifur elects the lie as an essential part of human existence. On page xiii of his introduction, Halldór gives a passage translated into English from the Icelandic version. The mood of the entire work can be exemplified by the following quotation from this passage: "See, in a word, all those exquisite things which human ingenuity has been able to invent, and art to produce. All this would nowhere be found if the lie had not entered the world; because men would then have lived like wild beasts in forests and fields, as they did once upon a time in Paradise, and neither used houses nor dress, nor any buildings." Actually, Halldór believed that the satire was "primarily directed against the story of the fall of man, which the Lutheran church treated as an historical fact" (p. xviii), although Þorleifur himself had been trained as a theologian and was at his early death rector of the cathedral school at Hólar. Halldór felt that Þorleifur's chief object was "to stimulate men to free and enlightened inquiry about human affairs, so that they might not blindly follow all they heard from the authorities" (ibid.). Be that as it may, the satire is indeed a contrast to the predominantly religious and ecclesiastical literature of the seventeenth and early eighteenth centuries, and is a welcome bit of evidence of the wit and humor that were undercurrents of life in Iceland and Denmark around 1700, despite the superficially rather dour impression that Lutheranism of that time otherwise makes.

Incidentally, Halldór's edition of this satire unwittingly gave him an opportunity to demonstrate his familiarity with medieval Latin literature and a command of the Latin language which enabled him to edit, as volume X of *Islandica* (1917), two Latin manuscripts by the one-time bishop of Skálholt, Gísli Oddsson (1593–1638): *Annalium in Islandia farrago* from the year 1637 and *De mirabilibus Islandiae* from the year 1638, both of which Halldór had located and examined in the Bodleian Library in Oxford. The manuscripts belong to that group of items which the early nineteenth-century scholar Finnur Magnússon had obtained from the Icelandic archivist Grímur Thorkelin and then sold to the Bodleian Library.

The two works appealed to Halldór Hermannsson both as examples of an enlightened man's productive intellectual efforts in the seventeenth century and as evidence of their author's patriotism and native pride. Halldór saw in the *Annalium farrago* a source of Icelandic folklore—which gave insight into the superstitious beliefs of the early seventeenth century, although not into those everyday events about which we often know less than we do about the grotesque ideas and extraordinary events of a time past.

The importance of *De mirabilibus* lies in the fact that it was a first attempt to describe the natural phenomena of Iceland. While not a little of Gísli's book is devoted to supernatural beings, it does give information about geography and the flora and fauna of Iceland, discusses in particular the birds, fish, insects, and animals of Iceland, and in addition provides considerable information on the place names of Iceland. The last five chapters are of historical importance, in that they, unlike the *Annalium farrago*, do indeed describe the daily life of the Icelanders of the time. Halldór tends to excuse Gísli his vagaries and superstitions because of the age in which he lived, and points out that Gísli was no more given to superstition and grotesque explanation than the other natural scientists of his time. Gísli, he wrote, "presents the outlook of an educated man of the seventeenth century on the nature surrounding him" (p. xiv). Halldór emphasizes that, for all its weaknesses and despite its brevity, *De mirabilibus* is the foremost work of its kind written by an Icelander in the seventeenth century.

Were it not for the fragments of the *Physiologus*, which owe their preservation to the tenaciousness of Árni Magnússon as a collector of manuscripts in the seventeenth century, there would be no evidence that one of the most popular medieval European books was also once found in an Icelandic version. The fragments must be taken to represent a kind of popular literature that existed in Iceland from the twelfth century onward but for which there is little documentary evidence. One must bear in mind that, despite the riches of the Arnamagnaean Collection, most medieval Icelandic manuscripts have been destroyed in the course of time, either by the hand of man, or by fire, or by loss at sea. One can only assume and hope that the preserved manuscripts are true indicators of the bulk of written literature that once existed in Iceland. It is not out of place to note analogously that, although the *Physiologus* originally was a Greek work, all the early manuscripts of the work which have been preserved are in Latin.

The *Physiologus* is better known as the *Bestiary*—the "Physiologus" *per se* would be the natural historian who compiled the book. As Halldór explains in his introduction to the Icelandic text contained in *The Icelandic Physiologus*

(*Islandica* XXVII, 1938), the *Bestiary* "popularized certain animals and their alleged characteristics and thus not only influenced the people at large, but also artists and writers" (p. 6). The *Physiologus* must have interested Halldór in particular because the animals it depicts are found again in many illuminated manuscripts (as well as in heraldry). Originally the animals were supposed to be of symbolic significance, but they soon evolved merely into decorative figures. Halldór suggests, however, that the symbolism derived from the *Physiologus* might be a subject worthy of further investigation.

The greatest importance of the *Physiologus*, Halldór explains, lies not in any literary or artistic virtue, but rather in its exemplification of the character of natural history around the year 1200 and in the fact that the *Physiologus*, which enjoyed a long and influential history on the Continent, reached Iceland at all; to our knowledge, it was not translated into any of the other Scandinavian languages. What is more, the Icelandic *Physiologus* is on the one hand the first work known to have dealt with natural history, whether fantastic or real, in Iceland and, on the other, the first illustrated book made in Iceland that is still extant. Halldór deplores the fact that the quality of the reproductions in his edition necessarily is poor because of the condition of the manuscript leaves themselves. Through photographic techniques developed in recent decades, however, these fragments could be reproduced more satisfactorily today.

The text that Halldór printed was a normalized rather than diplomatic one. Thus *þeirra* has replaced *þera*; *sefr*, *søfr*; *sannr*, *saþr*; and so forth. (The modern Icelandic form *grípendur* for *grípendr* was merely an oversight.) One concludes therefore that Halldór intended his edition of the *Physiologus* to contribute to intellectual history rather than to present a text for linguistic analysis. He did not lack interest in the Icelandic language—or more particularly in its historical development, as he had already addressed himself to that topic in 1919, in volume XII of *Islandica, Modern Icelandic: An Essay*.

Halldór Hermannsson's treatise on the modern Icelandic language is, however, as much a contribution to the general discussion of the development of Icelandic in the twentieth century, the relationship between Icelandic and Danish, and the desirability of introducing foreign terms into Icelandic as it is an historical analysis of the language per se. The essay is addressed to the educated general reader and is in part persuasive in tone; it does not attempt descriptions of the Icelandic grammars and dictionaries that were issued up to World War I.

The first part of the essay is given over to a discussion of the Icelandic language from the introduction of the Reformation into Iceland to the social and political changes of the eighteenth century. The seventeenth century in particular is described as an era of decline for the Icelandic language, whereas in the eighteenth century Icelandic was involved in a struggle with Danish for self-assertion. Halldór saw the real turning point in the history of the language in the work of the Danish philologist Rasmus Rask, who issued an intelligently organized grammar of Icelandic in 1811. Rask's work has been basic not only to the study of Icelandic but also to the development of Germanic philology ever since. He took an analytical approach to Germanic languages, rather than simply attempting to superimpose Latin paradigms on non-Latinate tongues.

Throughout his essay, Halldór passes judgment upon the quality of efforts to alter or improve Icelandic. He does not hesitate to call certain changes undesirable or to express subjective opinion about terms that he finds felicitous for phonetic or historical reasons. *Modern Icelandic* is prima facie evidence of Halldór's cultural nationalism—although he did not lose all objectivity about his native tongue. To the claims that there were no dialects in Iceland, for example, he had his reservations, although the differences that exist in modern Icelandic are not so great as to cause any difficulty in understanding between the inhabitants of one area and another.

He applauds those efforts, both philological and imaginative, that have contributed to "the improvement of style and the raising of literary taste" (p. 51). In this connection he mentions as noteworthy examples Jón Árnason's *Íslenzkar þjóðsögur og æfintýri*, narratives by Jón Thoroddsen and Einar Hjörleifsson Kvaran, and Steingrímur Thorsteinsson's translation of the *Arabian Nights*. Halldór stresses the pervasive importance of successful Icelandic translations of classical works, notably Sveinbjörn Egilsson's translations from Homer.

Halldór was skeptical about some of the puristic efforts in the sciences, and came to the conclusion that the advantages and disadvantages of using a foreign term or coining an Icelandic term must be weighed in every case. Some neologisms he found successful, others not. "Taken as a whole," he observes (p. 56), "the work done in this field is most remarkable, and shows, perhaps better than anything else, the richness of the language and its infinite possibilities in word formation."

His general position on language change was conservative. He advised against "sweeping changes in the orthography," since such changes would decrease the number of people able to read early prose literature without much difficulty (p. 63).

On one point his prognosis turned out to be incorrect. He felt that the system of patronymics eventually would have to be given up in Iceland since it had been abandoned elsewhere in Europe. The system became a matter of considerable national pride, if not chauvinism, for the Icelanders in the twentieth century, however, so that legislation has assured the continuance of the patronymic system to the present day.

Halldór felt that the forces of change could seriously affect the language of such a small nation as Iceland at a time when its isolation was lessening—even in 1919—and he spoke of a decrease in the linguistic "protection of former times" afforded by such isolation (p. 65). He nevertheless did not fear for the language, because the general level of education in Iceland had never been higher, and Iceland possessed a modern literature "richer and of a greater variety than ever before" (p. 66). He believed that the many national institutions in Iceland (and presumably in the first instance the new university) would help preserve and augment the traditions of the country and instill Icelanders with a reverence for their culture and a love of their language, which he identified as their "most precious possession"—reason enough for the Icelanders to strive to preserve it. The only real threat to the language he saw in a possible large immigration of foreigners. Actually, immigration to Iceland since Halldór wrote his essay has been small, but the influx of foreigners, that is to say American and British soldiers, during World War II was extremely large. Since a practical separation between Icelanders and the foreign soldiers was ultimately effected, the threat posed to the native tongue by so many speakers of English in Iceland was mitigated to a considerable extent, at least prior to the establishment of a television station at the American military base at Keflavik in the 1960's.

Halldór pointed out that under the impact of aviation, films, and radio, Icelandic culture would change rapidly and probably radically, and that it was therefore necessary to undertake without delay a thorough study of Icelandic culture as it had been preserved hitherto, as well as of the Icelandic language itself. He suggested that a historical dictionary of the Icelandic language be started—and this project subsequently came into being. Actually there are two lexicographical undertakings: a dictionary of the older language has been in preparation since 1939 in Copenhagen and historical dictionary of modern Icelandic has been in preparation since 1944 in Reykjavik, at the University of Iceland.

Halldór's vision of rapid change was prophetic indeed. Twenty-one years after he had published his volume on the Icelandic language, Iceland was occupied by foreign forces during World War II, and changes in civilization and culture that must be called radical began very soon to take place, so that, as Halldór would say metaphorically after the war, Iceland had been thrust from the nineteenth into the twentieth century almost overnight. Fortunately, Halldór Hermannsson had spoken in time as a scholar and a patriot and had been listened to. The seeds that he helped plant bore much fruit.

IV

Putting Iceland on the Map

As must now be evident, Halldór Hermannsson was instrumental in making available old documentary evidence pertaining to the description and history of Iceland. His motivation was historical, scholarly, and patriotic, but at the same time practical. Some of the material he edited in this connection was published for the first time; other material he made available for the first time in English. Several of the volumes of *Islandica* are concerned either directly or indirectly with the cartography of Iceland, notably *Islandica* XV–XVIII and XXI, beginning with the volume on Jón Guðmundsson in 1924 and ending with the volume devoted to the history of the cartography of Iceland in 1931.

Because the description of Iceland by Jón Guðmundsson (1574–c.1650) is the earliest treatise on the natural history of Iceland which has been preserved, Halldór elected to edit it, and in 1924 it was published in *Islandica* XV: *Jón Guðmundsson and His Natural History of Iceland.* In his introduction to the Icelandic text, Halldór presents Jón as rather a fantastic person given to both superstition and hallucinations, worried about the existence of devils and about persons practicing witchcraft against him. We learn that Jón himself was charged with witchcraft and blasphemy and was several times involved with the law. Indeed, he was outlawed in

Silhouette made in Tivoli Gardens, September 1923

1635 and, after fleeing to Copenhagen in 1636, was for a time imprisoned there. "It is clear that Jón did not enjoy a good reputation during his lifetime," Halldór notes dryly (p. xiii). Nevertheless, because Jón was of an inquisitive nature and made use of books, manuscripts, and documents that came his way, was familiar with Old Icelandic literature, and had a command of at least Danish and German in addition to Icelandic, he is an interesting person, although his works show him to have been uncritical and credulous. Several fragments of Jón's *Natural History of Iceland* existed in manuscript but had not previously been printed. Halldór put together his text on the basis of the fragments preserved in the National Library in Reykjavik, the Royal Library in Stockholm, and the Royal Library in Copenhagen.

Twelve pages of Halldór's notes in English provide a commentary to the Icelandic text. Jón had been familiar with whalers during his lifetime, and drew numerous pictures of whales; five of the nine plates in *Islandica* XV reproduce these drawings. Also reproduced is a copy of a map he made of the northern regions of Iceland (the original has been lost). Halldór printed the copy of the map both because it suggests the geographical concepts of Jón and his contemporaries, and because it seems to have drawn on various Old Icelandic sagas for some of its information.

Volume XVII, entitled *Two Cartographers: Guðbrandur Thorláksson and Thórður Thorláksson*, is Halldór Hermannsson's first essay into cartography. It is one of his shortest works—there are only forty-four pages of text and notes; in addition, the volume has nine plates reproducing various early maps of Iceland from the end of the fifteenth century through the second half of the seventeenth century. It is a curious fact, as Halldór points out, that the navigation of the Icelanders in the Middle Ages seems to have been carried out without the use of maps. In any case, there was no native cartography in early Iceland, and Halldór calls attention to the fact that the oldest maps preserved in Iceland are copies of foreign originals. Guðbrandur Þorláksson (1542–1627) was the first Icelandic cartographer. Since Guðbrandur was active as a clergyman and finally as a bishop, his concern with cartography could not have been a primary one, however. Þórður, who also became a bishop, was the great-grandson of Guðbrandur. Like his great-grandfather, he had—naturally—also studied in Copenhagen; while he was in Copenhagen, incidentally, he wrote a work on Greenland which is still preserved in manuscript in the Royal Library.

After examining the extant maps of Iceland, Halldór concluded that one could distinguish among three different types of configurations representing the island. The first goes back to the fifteenth-century Danish cartographer Claudius Clavus and is of a somewhat elongated island surrounded by smaller islands; a second is the so-called Fixlanda type (Halldór surmises that the name may be equated with "Fishland"), surprising in its fairly accurate representation of the indentations around the island; the third is the type represented by Olaus Magnus' *Carta marina*, published in Venice in 1539, in which the shape of the island is far less accurate than on the Fixlanda map.

Compared with the earliest efforts, the map ascribed to Guðbrandur is astonishing in its accuracy, as Halldór shows by reproducing it from an engraving dated 1585 and dedicated to the Danish scholar A. S. Vedel by the mapmaker Abraham Ortelius. Halldór notes that, although some of the place names seem to have been reworked in Danish fashion, "almost all of them are easily recognizable and clearly show that the original map was by an Icelander" (p. 16). Halldór examined all available maps of Iceland made by European cartographers in the sixteenth century, and could demonstrate that, ultimately, the model upon which all other cartographers drew was the Olaus Magnus map by way of Ortelius. Similarly, Gerhard Mercator's map from his 1595 *Atlas* is presumably based on the map Ortelius used as a model. Halldór compares the various maps and subtly demonstrates their interdependence. He advances the theory that Mercator obtained his map from Henrik Rantzau, a Danish nobleman who had furnished Mercator with information about Scandinavia, and points out that Rantzau was a patron of Vedel. As the most famous mapmaker of his time, Mercator and his map consequently became the authority and source of many other maps. Halldór traces the lineage of the maps through the seventeenth century.

The sources upon which Þórður Þorláksson drew is a vexing question. Halldór felt that, in Þórður's opinion, the Mercator map may have seemed the most reliable. In any case, Þórður's first map of Iceland, from the year 1668, most nearly resembles the Mercator map. Halldór is of the opinion that Bishop Þórður's third map (the second map has disappeared) is a more nearly original work, "quite remarkable for its time, artistically drawn, and often suprisingly accurate in detail" (p. 29). The map is the more admirable, says Halldór, since no trigonometrical survey of the country had been made, and any map would have to have been based upon personal observation or on written sources and astronomical measurements. Halldór concludes with regret that Þórður Þorláksson's less accurate maps were his best known and most widely imitated, whereas his third map of Iceland, the map that displays originality, "remained neglected and without influence upon cartography" (p. 38).

Halldór Hermannsson wrote no more thoroughly researched treatise than *The Cartography of Iceland* (*Islandica*

XXI, 1931) with which he concluded his series of studies pertaining to the cartography (and travel literature) of Iceland. By a sifting of both primary and secondary material relative to seamanship and nautical history, he sought out and described earlier sailing directions that pertained to Iceland and other countries. The footnotes in Halldór's treatise refer to an extensive literature in many languages including, of course, Latin and Italian, with both of which he felt at ease.

Twenty-six plates appended to the text reproduce the maps Halldór describes, ranging from an eleventh-century Anglo-Saxon map to Björn Gunnlaugsson's accurate representation of the island from the year 1849. Half the volume is devoted to primitive sailing directions and early maps, chiefly of the sixteenth century. The other half deals with the maps of the eighteenth and nineteenth centuries.

Halldór reminds us that there was gross ignorance of Iceland at the time the earliest maps were drawn, a fact that explains some of the grotesquely inaccurate representations of the island prior to the second half of the sixteenth century. Halldór had cast a broad net and identified maps of varying provenance. He pays particular attention to the map of the fourteenth-century Danish cartographer Claudius Clavus since other mapmakers seem to have drawn on Clavus and since the accompanying text contains place names. As exemplified by the world map of the great cartographer Gerhard Mercator in 1554, the concept of the shape of Iceland—not to mention the interior of the country which was not described at all until the eighteenth century—was even then rather inaccurate.

Halldór describes all sources of Icelandic cartography up to the first half of the sixteenth entury and touches also upon the question whether Columbus may have obtained information about navigation to North America from Icelandic sources, without, however, taking any position in the matter. He interprets each of the maps mentioned in an endeavor to define the possible interrelationship and interdependence of the maps. Halldór's treatment of cartography from the second half of the sixteenth century onward is more summary because of the larger amount of material extant but also in certain instances because some items were not available for his perusal. Halldór focuses on Dutch cartographers, and again with special reference to one Joris Carolus of Enkhuyzen—who turns out to be identical with the "Georgus Carolus Flandrus" whom Halldór had mentioned in his *Two Cartographers of Iceland* in 1926. In assessing the earlier maps, Halldór suggests that phonetic variation in the transmission of place names on maps might lead to important conclusions regarding the origins and provenance of some maps and also the probable nationality of some of the cartographers themselves.

The second half of *The Cartography of Iceland* discusses contributions from the eighteenth and nineteenth centuries. Halldór's presentation, while based on the same principles that inform the first half of the book, is concerned primarily with Danish maps, French coastal surveys and hydrography, and, finally, the decisive labors of the two Icelanders Björn Gunnlaugsson and Þorvaldur Thoroddsen. Halldór accounts for various expeditions to Iceland and into Icelandic waters sent by the Danish and French governments and also by the Danish Academy of Sciences. He recognizes, in particular, the importance of the map completed in 1734 by the Norwegian army officer T. H. H. Knopf, who had spent four years in Iceland taking measurements and whose map was "for nearly a century . . . the standard map of the country upon which all other map-makers drew" (p. 48). Halldór concludes his survey with mention of the modern scientific triangulation and geodetic survey of Iceland that was begun at the turn of the twentieth century by the authority of the Icelandic Althing and the geodetic section of the Danish General Staff—and that had not yet been completed at his time of writing in 1931.

Halldór's interest in the cartography of Iceland had as a matter of course led him to an examination of works on description and travel, some of which also had a direct bearing on cartography. Eggert Ólafsson (1726–68), a noted topographer, became the subject of a biographical treatise published in 1925 as volume XVI of *Islandica*. The first section of *Eggert Ólafsson* sketches the history of Iceland from its submission to the king of Norway in the thirteenth century to the beginning of the eighteenth century. As he did on so many other occasions, Halldór—although kindly disposed toward twentieth-century Denmark—stresses the maladministration of Iceland from Copenhagen, especially in the sixteenth and seventeenth centuries, and implies that cultural and even political independence is highly desirable. He saw in Eggert Ólafsson a patriot and savior of the country, who appeared on the scene when Iceland's "very existence hung in the balance" (p. 7). Eggert Ólafsson appealed to Halldór in part because Eggert was a man of many interests and made a substantial contribution in several fields—like Halldór himself. Moreover, Eggert was one of those travelers through Iceland who left invaluable written documentation of what he saw and examined. Halldór was particularly impressed by Eggert's attention to the geology and flora of Iceland.

Halldór Hermannsson observes that in the records of his travels, Eggert Ólafsson provides us with unmatched examples of cultural history from the eighteenth century. To make his point, Halldór includes a couple of pages of description of a country wedding in which Eggert had participated.

Eggert Ólafsson's journey through Iceland had been undertaken with the most prestigious support—that of the Royal Academy of Sciences in Copenhagen. The report on Eggert's trip was issued in two volumes by the Academy in 1772. Originally written in the Danish language, it appeared in German translation within two years. Eggert was not only a traveler and topographer, but also a poet—although most of the poems were not printed until several decades after his death. Halldór discusses them in some detail, since the poems are of historical importance and are widely known in Iceland. Despite Halldór's affinity with Eggert Ólafsson, he was under no illusion regarding the eighteenth-century writer's poetic gifts: "The poems are sensible, logical, even impressive, nay, inspiring at times," but they "are frequently unaesthetic, and show lack of good taste now and then." Halldór describes Eggert's poetic vein as "more a product of cultivation than a natural product" (p. 29). Halldór recognized that Eggert's poems were nevertheless a "new departure in Icelandic literature" since they describe the nature and beauties of the country, "the amusements and occupations appertaining to the different seasons, the plants and the animals which both give a joy to the eye and food for the body" (p. 32). Considerable space is devoted to the poem "Búnaðarbálkur," which appeared separately in 1783. Halldór concludes that the poem must have been modeled in part on Albrecht von Haller's German "Die Alpen" and in part on Christian B. Tullin's Norwegian "Majdagen," both of which praise the virtues of the rural life and came to enjoy the status of modern classics.

Halldór summarizes Eggert Ólafsson's concern for the Icelandic language and his writings on that subject—a matter he had touched upon previously in volume XII of *Islandica, Modern Icelandic.* It is amusing to note that the characteristics and virtues of Eggert Ólafsson which Halldór extolls at the end of the biography are to a large extent those Halldór shared with Eggert: "He was a tall man, handsome of face, strongly built, . . . resolute, somewhat grave, yet in daily intercourse cheerful. He was complete master of his emotions in joy and sorrow . . . . He loved his native land and never was in agreement with those who . . . sought to enrich themselves at its expense . . . Popular prejudices and errors he tried to eradicate. All his life he kept aloof from quarrels among men, only interfering when he saw the possibility of settling them or bringing about reconciliation. This indeed is an engaging picture" (pp. 53–54). And this is very nearly a description that persons who knew Halldór Hermannsson recognize as applicable to him.

Halldór's love of his native country is particularly evident in the first paragraph of his biography of Eggert Ólafsson. After mentioning the glaciers of Iceland he adds, "They are impressive, to be sure, and will long be remembered by one who has once seen them. But the name [Iceland] leaves out the blue mountains and the green hills and valleys which also will linger in the memory of the traveller, not to speak of the numerous volcanoes which represent the very element opposed to ice." And in a different mood he remarks of the Icelanders: "Strong hands are required here to grapple with nature and make her yield sustenance to men, and only by hard struggle have they managed to live there for ten centuries."

Perhaps in part because Halldór Hermannsson felt at home in London, he was particularly attracted to the figure of Sir Joseph Banks, the English scholar and traveler who made an expedition to Iceland in 1772—and who became the subject of *Islandica* XVIII (1928): *Sir Joseph Banks and Iceland.*

Since Sir Joseph Banks's own notes on the trip to Iceland in the summer of 1772 were thought to have been lost,[1] Halldór found it necessary to reconstruct the story of his journey to and through the island from both British and Scandinavian collateral sources. Sir Joseph had been accompanied by some forty other persons, including the Swede Uno von Troil (later Archbishop of Uppsala), who in 1777 published a lengthy if rather misleading description of the trip. For *Islandica* XVIII, Halldór examined with great thoroughness the sources that could contribute to his dissertation and was consequently able to tell a coherent tale of Banks's sojourn in Iceland. He determined that the ship Sir Joseph had chartered left England on the twelfth of July 1772, arrived in Iceland on the twenty-eighth of August, and departed again on the fifteenth of October. The Icelandic sources in particular make clear the warmth with which the Icelanders received Sir Joseph. Subsequent correspondence with Icelanders, and notably with the government official Ólafur Stephensen, attests Sir Joseph Banks's continued kindly and appreciative attitude toward Iceland and its inhabitants. Time and again he endeavored to be of some assistance to Icelanders—and Sir Joseph was, after all, a

[1] The papers of Sir Joseph Banks had a complex fate; they were ultimately sold and scattered. The Icelandic journal was acquired in December 1924 by the Blacker-Wood Library of Zoology and Ornithology at McGill University in Montreal, but its whereabouts remained unknown for many years. The journal was recently published by Roy A. Rauschenberg as "The Journal of Joseph Banks' Voyage up Great Britain's West Coast to Iceland and to the Orkney Isles, July to October, 1772," in *Proceedings of the American Philosophical Society* 117 (1973), 186–226. On the whole, the journal—which was carelessly written and is incomplete—corroborates Halldór Hermannsson's narrative, although some details augment it.

man of great influence. He was not only wealthy, but a member, and for over forty years the president, of the Royal Society.

Halldór felt that the most valuable evidence preserved from the Banks expedition were the sketches and engravings made by three artists who accompanied Sir Joseph to Iceland: the brothers J. F. and James Miller and John Clevely. Twenty-four plates appended to Halldór's text reproduce work by the Millers and Clevely and provide a unique insight into certain conditions of the country in the year 1772, for many natives in contemporary dress and houses appear in these pictures.

At the beginning of the nineteenth century certain events took place which, Halldór discovered, again involved Sir Joseph Banks with Iceland, although only at a distance. In Sir Joseph's correspondence (preserved in the Museum of Natural History in London) Halldór located a lengthy paper he presumed was intended for the British government, entitled "Remarks concerning Iceland" and dated 30 January 1801. The ultimate intent of the paper was to argue for British annexation of Iceland at a time when Denmark had allied herself with Russia, Sweden, and Prussia and was threatening British commerce. From the tone of the paper, which Halldór reprints in full on pages 25–30, it is clear that Sir Joseph Banks continued to be kindly disposed to Iceland and believed that British annexation could only be advantageous to the island. He wrote, for example, that Britain "could emancipate from an Egyptian bondage a population consisting entirely of fishermen, and consequently seamen, that would rapidly increase under her mild government" (p. 29). The British government did not act on Sir Joseph's suggestion. Halldór also located a letter from Sir Joseph to Ólafur Stephensen, which was to be put in the latter's hands after the British had taken over but was never delivered.

Later Sir Joseph received a letter from Ólafur Stephensen's son Magnús, written in October of 1807, requesting Sir Joseph's intervention to help four Icelandic merchant ships that had been brought to Britain as an act of war. Further letters found in Sir Joseph's correspondence indicate that he indeed did make vigorous efforts to help the sequestered ships and finally effected their release.

A second matter involved Sir Joseph Banks somewhat inadvertently and was not to his liking. This concerns the caper of the Danish adventurer, Jörgen Jörgensen, who went on a British ship to Iceland in 1809 and attempted to set up a government and ultimately proclaim himself king of the island. As is well known, he was unsuccessful in his venture and was subsequently imprisoned in England. Jörgensen called upon Sir Joseph Banks after returning from Iceland, but it is not clear what passed between them. Very soon, at least, Sir Joseph's attitude toward him was demonstrably unfavorable, and despite various pleas from Jörgensen and from the botanist William Jackson Hooker on his behalf, Sir Joseph made no effort to aid Jörgensen (who ultimately was sent to Tasmania as a convict).

Halldór Hermannsson felt that it was only because of the influence and respect Sir Joseph commanded that the British government finally declared Iceland neutral in February of 1810. There followed a renewed suggestion that Great Britain should annex Iceland. Halldór unearthed some further notes "relative to the ancient State of Iceland" in which Sir Joseph Banks had had a hand, although this time he was not their author—notes that apparently had been drawn up for submission to the British government or some member thereof. Halldór concludes that although various English statesmen had toyed with the idea of annexing Iceland, the government never took any action in this matter because such an annexation would not be to the advantage of

England. Nothing would be gained, except temporarily, in attempting to humiliate Denmark by taking away part of the kingdom. In retrospect Halldór weighs the advantages and disadvantages of British annexation in the Napoleonic era and concludes that annexation probably would have meant Anglicization of the island with a subsequent loss of Icelandic language and traditions, but adds that "it is always idle to speculate about what course history might have taken under certain conditions" (p. 98). In conclusion he speaks with affection of Sir Joseph Banks's interest in and admiration for Iceland as probably contributing to the appreciation of Icelandic literature that grew markedly in England during the nineteenth century.

V

The Vinland Question

A subject that attracted Halldór Hermannsson's interest repeatedly after his removal to the New World was the literature regarding the discovery and brief settlement of some part of the coast of North America by Scandinavians around the year 1000. He lost no time in addressing himself to it, and volume II of *Islandica* (1909) accounted for this literature in a bibliography entitled *The Northmen in America (982–c. 1500)*, and thus laid the groundwork for future research as well as for an assessment of the many speculative contributions to the question that had appeared before 1909. Like Willard Fiske, Halldór was skeptical about the value of most of the extant literature on the subject. In his preface to the bibliography he says, "Even many works professing to treat the subject seriously, must be looked upon as products of pure imagination." He did not himself write an extensive treatise on the subject before 1936, when he published a critical—and speculative—essay entitled *The Problem of Wineland*, as *Islandica* XXV. In 1930 he had acted as general editor of Matthías Þórðarson's *The Vinland Voyages* published in English translation by the American Geographical Society, a volume to which Vilhjalmur Stefansson provided an introduction. Later, in *The Vinland Sagas* (*Islandica* XXX, 1944), he reedited the most important texts preserved in Old Icelandic which pertain to the Vinland voyages.

Halldór also wrote several articles on the Vinland voyages for various periodicals, both popular and scholarly, partly anticipating his arguments of the year 1936. Two of these appeared in *The Geographical Review*, the first in volume XVII (1927), "The Wineland Voyages: A Few Suggestions" (pp. 107–14), and the second in volume XXIII (1933), "The Norsemen's Farthest North in Greenland" (pp. 334–35). A summary of his views about the medieval Icelanders and North America was published in the international journal *Le Nord* in 1940, under the title "The Vinland Voyages." This article, like the two articles in Icelandic which he wrote for the Icelandic-American periodical *Tímarit Þjóðræknisfélags Íslendinga* in 1932 and 1941, the first on Leif the Lucky, and the other on Columbus and Cabot, merely present the evidence, and state Halldór Hermannsson's case without bringing any new basic information. In 1940 he also contributed the article on "Vinland" to the *Encyclopaedia Britannica* which was included in the reprintings of the encyclopedia through 1966. As late as 1954, at the age of seventy-six, he published an article on the figure of the German-born Tyrkir in *Modern Language Notes* (Vol. LXIX, pp. 388–93).

No work by Halldór Hermannsson called forth more reviews than did *The Problem of Wineland.* Unlike many other volumes of *Islandica*, it was not primarily bibliographical, textual or factual, but was a contribution to a vigorously—sometimes hotly—disputed question, an interpretation of documents upon which there is no concensus, and an attempt to establish a reasonable hypothesis regarding the voyages of the Icelanders—or "Norsemen"—to the North American continent around the year 1000. Halldór's presentation is based entirely upon written evidence as it has been preserved in Icelandic codices; he willfully disregarded the highly questionable archeological evidence that had been brought forward abundantly and profusely for a century and a half. The several reviewers of the work were favorably impressed by it. Some remarks in the *Times Literary Supplement* in London on 20 March 1937 (p. 202) exemplify the reception Halldór's study received and may be quoted here: "The sanity of this book makes it a most refreshing contrast to much rubbish which has been printed about the Norse discovery of America. Mr. Hermannsson's close study of the evidence, his sound critical judgment, and his broad common sense render his conclusions particularly worthy of respect." And Angus MacDonald, writing in the *Modern Language Review* (XX [1937], 489), called it a "comprehensive, readable and scholarly work." This paean of praise was evoked by Halldór's rational attempt at objective evaluation of the story of the discovery of North America as contained in the saga literature. He set out simply to answer the question: what must we conclude if we accept the evidence in the sagas?

The Problem of Wineland retells the story of the voyages as contained both in *Eiríks saga rauða* and *Grœnlendinga þáttr*. At some points the two reports are in disagreement, and there is even some internal inconsistency and ambivalence. In such cases, one must simply rely upon common sense and good judgment in an attempt to explain what the sagas actually say—as indeed Halldór did.

Having presented all the documentary evidence and having dismissed the misleading or pseudo-archeological evidence such as the Newport Tower and the infamous Kensington Stone, Halldór draws some warranted conclusions about the route the Scandinavian seamen must have taken between Greenland and the North American continent, and also about the location of places they visited and temporarily settled. This investigation was, of course, a kind of detective work, and remained consciously within the realm of hypothesis. A decade previously Halldór had nurtured the hope of exploring the coast of northern North America and Labrador together with Vilhjalmur Stefansson, but this plan came to naught. It was with such a voyage in mind he had written his article for *The Geographical Review* in 1927. *The Problem of Wineland* was an extension and variation of the ideas Halldór had expressed there. In the earlier article, he had called for a physical examination of the North American coast with a concomitant effort to determine which parts of the coast jibed with the descriptions in the Icelandic sources. Central to his argument in both the article and in *The Problem of Wineland* was the identification of the seventy-five-mile-long Chaleur Bay on the Gaspé Peninsula as the Straumfjord of the saga. The bay contains an island (Heron Island) that could be the Straumey, and would have been reached by sailing down the coast of Labrador; the area north of Hamilton Inlet could be identified as Helluland, and the area south as Markland. The harborless and sandy coast of southeast and southern Labrador could then correspond to the Furðustrands of the Icelandic text. Vinland would have been reached by sailing around Nova Scotia and along the coast of New Brunswick to the shore of New England, someplace west and south of Passamaquoddy Bay. Halldór did not attempt to place Hóp at any specific place in New England because of the paucity of detailed information and the variable factor of changes in climate. He points out, however, that the Icelandic sources do not state that Hóp was in Vinland. He looks to ethnology and archeology to furnish further information on the tribes that the Icelanders met nearly a thousand years ago. All in all, Halldór's is a reasonable theory and cannot be said to have been disproved any more than it has been demonstrated in the half century since he first proposed it.

Halldór reflected at some length on the possible connections between the discovery of America by the Icelanders on the one hand and the discoveries by Columbus and Cabot on the other. Columbus, according to the biography of his son, visited Iceland in 1477. A description contained in a seventeenth-century Spanish document regarding a part of the world that has been identified as Thule may or may not have been written by Columbus and may or may not refer to Iceland. All this is very tenuous; we simply do not know whether any information of the earlier voyages reached Columbus, and therefore whether the Icelanders can be connected with the late fifteenth-century discovery of the New World. Halldór points out that there was a more plausible channel of information to the Cabots than to Columbus, through the city of Bristol, England, since Bristol kept up a commerce with Iceland. While these possibilities cannot be entirely dismissed, Halldór himself considered them hypothetical and not demonstrable on the basis of available information.

In the other volume of *Islandica* devoted to the matter of Vinland (XXX, 1944), Halldór printed a normalized text of *Eiríks saga rauða* and the chapters of *Ólafs saga Tryggvasonar* (the *Flateyjarbók* version) which constitute *Grœnlendinga þáttr*, but with footnotes indicating all textual variants on the basis of the extant manuscripts. He added several pages of explanatory notes to each of the selections. As an appendix (pp. 66–69), he printed passages from those other Icelandic works—from the *Íslendingabók* to sixteenth-century Icelandic annals—which contain some mention of the voyages of discovery to Vinland. A fourteen-page introduction discusses some of the literature that had appeared since the publication *The Problem of Wineland* in 1936 and several aspects of the saga literature containing the textual material in the volume. Halldór tried to steer a middle course between those critics who would accept the sagas of Icelanders as trustworthy historical sources and those who would look upon them as pure fiction. While Halldór believed that oral tradition had a better chance of preservation in Iceland than in most places, he felt that it would be "without a parallel if oral tradition had kept absolutely uncorrupted for two hundred years or more" (p. iii) a given text, although he felt that poetry may have been preserved because of its rigid form. In addition he briefly describes the manuscripts that served as his sources and in so doing expresses his opinion that most of the saga material was written down during the thirteenth century.

In his previous writings on the Vinland question, Halldór Hermannsson had cast considerable doubt upon the validity of the *Grœnlendinga þáttr* as preserved in the fourteenth-century *Flateyjarbók*. He now developed an argument that would further weaken the validity of the *Grœnlendinga þáttr* as an historical source. He points to the story of the voyage of one Snæbjörn Galti to the east coast of Greenland as described in the *Landnámabók*, and suggests that the voyage of Freydís is based on that story. While this is a striking observation, the conclusions that can be drawn from it are uncertain, and Halldór's theorizing about the shifting role of Freydís in tradition, and the peculiar description of the battle with the American Indians in *Eiríks saga rauða*, is not very convincing and cannot be said to make "certain that this separate voyage of hers is entirely without a foundation in facts" as he thought it would.

In addition to the publications already mentioned, Halldór reviewed books on the subject of the Icelandic discovery of America for learned periodicals. Incidentally, in a review of G. M. Gathorne-Hardy's *The Norse Discovery of America*, 1921, in *Isis*, volume IV (1922), Halldór objected to calling the early Scandinavian explorers "Norse," for, as he points out, to most people that term suggests Norway and Norwegians. He adds, "So far as we know, they were, however, all natives of Iceland, except Erik the Red, and his part in these voyages was inconsequential. They should therefore be called Icelandic." Strictly speaking, he is right, since we date the establishment of the separate Icelandic commonwealth from the year 930; the country did not come under the domination of Norway until the thirteenth century. It is probable, however, that the Icelandic discoverers of Greenland and North America will continue to be referred to as Norsemen since that term is so widespread in the literature.

Halldór changed his mind regarding the use of the anglicized term "Wineland" and reverted to using "Vinland." The treatment of Icelandic place names is, we observe, always a tricky one; many Icelandic place names have clear-cut meanings, and by retaining the Icelandic name one may fail to communicate its denotation. Nevertheless, translating a place name in order to explain it leads to confusion on several counts—the translation does not appear on any map, and translations made by different persons are not always identical. Although this was scarcely the case with the word "Vinland," Halldór felt on reflection that it would be wisest to retain the Icelandic term, probably because the translated form overemphasizes the concept of wine or grape-bearing vines, which is not really central in a discussion of the early Scandinavian voyages to North America.

When Halldór Hermannsson was invited to give a series of lectures by the University of Iceland in September 1938, he chose the Vinland voyages as his topic and gave three public lectures (September 5, 7, and 9). They were held in the Odd Fellows' Hall in Reykjavik—since the university auditorium was not large enough to accommodate the audience that the topic and the speaker were sure to attract.

VI

Manuscript Matters

Halldór Hermannsson was interested not only in printed books and their history, but also in manuscripts, although the Fiske Icelandic Collection is not and was not meant to be a collection of manuscripts. It is impossible, however, to be a scholar or otherwise active in the field of Old Norse–Icelandic studies without having to do with the manuscripts that in themselves preserve the treasure of Icelandic antiquities and provide the ultimate basis for textual scholarship. Moreover, the physical condition of the manuscripts and more particularly their illuminations were of great interest to Halldór, just as the physical condition of a book and its illustrations were of interest to him. Especially because of his close association with the Arnamagnaean Collection in Copenhagen, Halldór was well acquainted with the corpus of preserved Icelandic manuscripts and their monumental significance.

Both the general history of these priceless documents and the problems associated with them are the subject of a trenchant and in part impassioned discussion in volume XIX of *Islandica* in 1929: *Icelandic Manuscripts*. Halldór describes the introduction of writing into Iceland and provides some information on almost every facet of the manuscripts: the nature of the alphabet employed, the attempt to write Ice-

Halldór Hermannsson crossing City Hall Square, Copenhagen, 11 August 1928

landic phonetically, the composition of the ink, and the kind of parchment employed for the vellums. After mentioning those early Icelandic authors who are known by name, Halldór examines the Icelandic church inventories from the twelfth century onward in order to draw some conclusions regarding early collections of books in Iceland and, in particular, the relationship between religious and secular interest in Icelandic literature. In so doing, he was following the lead of the Swedish scholar Emil Olmer, who (in 1902) had written on the subject of early Icelandic book collecting. Although Halldór calls the obtainable information about early libraries "incomplete and unsatisfactory," he felt justified in drawing the conclusion that the secular literature of Iceland was not of clerical origin "and moreover that the manuscripts of this literature in no notable degree were preserved in the libraries of religious institutions" (p. 35). One may observe that the question of clerical versus nonclerical origins of Old Icelandic literature has still to be elucidated fully and that, in point of fact, some of the information Halldór includes in his study of Icelandic manuscripts can be used for arguing either side of the case. The second part of the essay is a *bibliographie raisonnée* for many of the 700 Icelandic manuscripts written before 1550 which are still preserved. In this second half of Halldór's book is found the sorry tale of the Icelandic manuscripts in modern times, with special emphasis upon the many efforts to collect and preserve manuscripts in the seventeenth century—efforts that came to mean the gradual exportation of almost all Icelandic manuscripts from Iceland and the subsequent destruction of many manuscripts, principally in a series of fires. Halldór reminds his reader that the seventeenth century in particular educed antiquarian interest in Iceland and that for this reason numerous Icelandic manuscripts were taken to Sweden, although by far the largest number of manuscripts was taken to Denmark, either by agents of the Danish king or by Danes or Icelanders themselves. While Árni Magnússon may be looked upon as the single most important collector of manuscripts, he was by no means one of the earliest. In fact, as Halldór points out, "with Árni Magnússon comes to an end the collecting of early Icelandic manuscripts. He had virtually scoured the country, so that very little was left" (p. 69). Halldór removes something of the nimbus surrounding the origin of the Arnamagnaean Collection by explaining that the decision regarding the disposition of the collection was made only a matter of days before Árni died in 1730, and that he left to the executors of his will the task of determining the conditions governing his bequest. Most of what Halldór has to say here is apparently the result of his studies during his stewardship of the Arnamagnaean Collection in Copenhagen during the academic year 1925/26. In retrospect, this part of the essay may be looked upon as preliminary to Halldór's later edition of the *Codex Frisianus* (1932) and of the folio devoted to Icelandic illuminated manuscripts (1935), both of which were published in the series *Corpus codicum Islandicorum medii aevi*. He also touches upon the *Jónsbók*, to which he was to devote some space in the work on illuminated manuscripts and then go on to describe in greater detail in a separate volume of *Islandica* in 1940.

As early as 1918, in his essay on Willard Fiske contained in the *Papers of the Bibliographical Society of America*, Halldór had expressed his basic agreement with Fiske's belief that manuscripts should stay in the countries of their origins, where they would be of most use. This principle was to become a matter of somewhat acrimonious debate a few decades later with regard to the Icelandic manuscripts preserved in Copenhagen. For the year 1929, Halldór was expressing himself forcibly on the general matter of Icelandic manuscripts when he wrote, on page 70 of volume XIX of *Islandica*, "The large production of manuscripts in Iceland is indeed remarkable and without parallel in history when the small number of population is taken into consideration; but equally unparalleled in the history of civilized nations is the wholesale exportation of manuscripts from the country, by which the nation was deprived practically of all its literary products of several centuries." He counters the argument that the manuscripts were saved by being sent abroad and notably to Denmark. While this may have been true in some cases, "it is an open question whether much was gained by it," he remarks—since so many manuscripts came to grief in Denmark in the eighteenth century. Halldór's attitude and arguments were to be taken over and reinforced by many of his countrymen twenty to thirty years later in a drawn-out—and ultimately successful—effort to obtain the return of Icelandic manuscripts to Iceland, since the manuscripts had been removed to Denmark on the authority of the king and, one might add, primarily for venal reasons.

To *Icelandic Manuscripts* there is appended a bibliography of catalogues of Icelandic manuscripts preserved in Iceland, Denmark, Sweden, Great Britain, Ireland, and France. In addition there are eight plates; the first shows an example of early Icelandic bookbinding, while the others reproduce pages of the major manuscripts mentioned in the text.

Complementing the essay on Icelandic manuscripts—*Islandica* XIX—is volume XXIII of *Islandica* (1933), entitled *Old Icelandic Literature: A Bibliographical Essay*. It describes the widespread interest in Old Icelandic literature in several countries and the history of the publication of that literature from the sixteenth through the first decades of the twentieth century. Most important in this volume, however, is the epilogue on pages 42–50 which made some specific suggestions about how Old Norse–Icelandic literature should be dealt with in the future and about a possible reformation of the Arnamagnaean Commission (established in 1730) which, in Halldór's words, had become a "rather inactive body" (p. 47). He had already spoken on this matter in an article in the Icelandic literary annual *Skírnir* in 1929. Halldór suggested specifically that the membership in the commission should be changed so that it consisted of an equal number of Danes and Icelanders, that the commission should underwrite the publication of critical editions and translations, preferably in one of the international languages, and that the commission should issue a periodical publication that would include "reviews, essays, or studies" (p. 48). He also suggested that the commission gather together a special library devoted to Old Icelandic literature. His suggestions struck a responsive chord in Denmark and Iceland and most were carried out within a relatively short time.

Very soon after the publication of *Islandica* XXIII, some Danish scholars, notably Carl S. Petersen, head of the Royal Library in Copenhagen, and Lis Jacobsen, administrator of the Danish Literary Society, again brought up the possibility of Halldór Hermannsson's becoming the custodian of the Arnamagnaean Collection. Once more, Halldór was not uninterested in the position if the remuneration were satisfactory and if subsidies would guarantee scholarly publication. That the matter was dropped for a second time suggests that a solution of the pecuniary question could not be found. The new serial publication for which Halldór had agitated was established in 1941, however. It bears the title *Bibliotheca Arnamagnaeana*, and has been edited by Jón Helgason and published by Ejnar Munksgaard. Halldór (who remained an Icelandic citizen to his death) was made a member of the reconstituted Arnamagnaean Commission in 1935. He attended several meetings of the commission in

1937 and 1939, but was unable to participate actively in the work of the commission thereafter, first because of World War II and later because of poor health that kept him from returning to Copenhagen. He resigned from the commission in 1952.

In the preface to volume XXVI of *Islandica* in 1937, Halldór could report that the reorganized Arnamagnaean Commission was planning to publish uniform editions of the mythical-heroic sagas of Iceland and had plans to issue the later fictitious sagas. He also noted that the commission was planning an Icelandic-English dictionary that would cover the period through the middle of the sixteenth century, and he expressed the hope that the dictionary might be completed in the course of ten years. While these plans were changed somewhat, a dictionary of Old Norse–Icelandic did get under way; since 1946 it has been under the supervision of Ole Widding.

Noteworthy is Halldór's defense of the native romantic sagas as a subject for scholarly endeavor. He says in his preface of the year 1937, "Insignificant or unimportant though many of them may appear to be, they are as a whole far from being negligible," for they "represent a characteristic feature of the literary activity of the Icelanders, that of writing, paraphrasing, and translating sagas" (p. vi). Since Halldór had several times attempted to call attention to the existence of a widespread popular literature derived from Continental sources and introduced into Iceland during the Middle Ages, it is worth noting that he greeted the publication of Margaret Schlauch's *Romance in Iceland* in 1934 with satisfaction, for here for the first time the many stories of adventure which are pejoratively known as *Lygisögur* are given their just due.

Halldór's first major essay into paleography was his edition of the *Codex Frisianus: Ms. No. 45 Fol. in the Arnamagnaean*

Collection) as volume IV in the series *Corpus codicum Islandicorum medii aevi*, in 1932. *Codex Frisianus* derives its singular eminence from the fact that it is the most important vellum manuscript of *Heimskringla*. It also contains an abridgment of Sturla Þórðarson's *Hákonar saga gamla Hákonarsonar*. The entire codex is, in Halldór Hermannsson's words, "a specimen of the efforts of fourteenth-century scribes to bring together, or to present, within the covers of one volume, a continuous history of the Norwegian Kings, by copying the various Kings' Sagas, generally in a somewhat abridged form" (Introd., p [1]). The *Codex Frisianus* includes the first and last parts of such a history but omits the saga of Saint Olaf the King. Since this omission cannot have been accidental, Halldór surmised that the person for whom the *Codex Frisianus* was compiled must already have possessed a copy of that saga.

The *Codex Frisianus* is striking because it contains history as written by two of the outstanding historians of medieval Iceland, Snorri Sturluson, the author of *Heimskringla*, and Sturla Þórðarson, the author of *Hákonar saga gamla*. The situations of the two writers were different: "Snorri wrote of the past which could be viewed at a distance and in perspective. His sources were limited, and he could give his imagination freer reins, and use all his literary skill in accordance with the best tradition of Icelandic story-telling. Sturla wrote of the immediate past and present, was supplied with plentiful material which could not be easily sifted, and where it was often difficult to discuss what was of importance and what transitory. To such matter he could not apply very successfully the old method of story-telling" (p. [8]).

Halldór concludes that the *Codex Frisianus* must have been written about 1325. He inclines to the opinion that the spelling and handwriting are Icelandic but notes that there are Norwegianisms in the language. He therefore does not take a definite stand on the provenance of the manuscript but claims it safe to assume it had been made for a Norwegian, "probably a member of the royal family, or of the aristocracy, or a high ecclesiastic" (p. [10])—a safe hypothesis in view of the great labor and cost that must have been involved in producing the manuscript.

In his introduction Halldór rejects the suggestion made by Guðbrandur Vigfússon that the *Codex Frisianus* was derived from Ari's lost book of kings. Halldór writes that there is no evidence for such a hypothesis and observes, "We are not in a position to estimate Snorri's debt to Ari" (p. [3]).

Particular attention is paid to the condition of the *Hákonar saga* in the *Codex Frisianus* because the codex contains only about three-fifths of the saga as otherwise known. Halldór observes that generally the scribe had "summarized, shortened or entirely omitted speeches" (p. [8]), although there are cases where the codex supplements the other texts. While Halldór guesses that in some instances the omissions can possibly be ascribed to that phenomenon known as homoioteleuton—sections of the story ending in similar ways (thus making it easy for a scribe to skip over a section of the manuscript)—neither he nor any other scholar has been able to explain the reasons for the shortening of the *Hákonar saga*, which in Halldór's words must be counted "among the first historical books of the Middle Ages" (p. [8]).

Halldór's most spectacular publication is the folio volume *Icelandic Illuminated Manuscripts of the Middle Ages* (1935), which is the seventh volume in the series *Corpus codicum Islandicorum medii aevi* issued by Ejnar Munksgaard in Copenhagen. The tome includes eighty plates containing 165 illustrations reproduced from Icelandic manuscripts, the oldest of which dates from about the year 1200. The first ten plates are in color; three reproduce full pages from as many manuscripts; the other color illustrations are chiefly of illuminated capitals. The photo-lithographic reproductions found on the remaining plates are about equally divided between full pages and portions of pages selected to show illuminations, primarily of initials.

In his introduction to the book, Halldór first discusses the origin of Icelandic script and the general history of manuscripts in Iceland. He evinces an astonishing familiarity with old Scandinavian history and sources pertaining to it. The introduction combines a knowledge of art history, archeology, philology, and bibliology, as well as history in general. On the basis of the many facts at his command, Halldór establishes a number of original hypotheses that are still tenable forty years after he first proposed them. He gathered bits of information from many sources in order to interpret the material with which he was working and to achieve an integrated presentation. He gives a thorough and detailed description of the illustrations, which he explains imaginatively but incisively. He discusses the probable origins of the models for the illustrations, and comes to the conclusion that most of the illuminations must have been based directly on English and French work, although some may have been transmitted to Iceland through Norway, as previously had been surmised. Halldór wrote with enthusiasm about the illustrations, the beauties of which he was able to discern because he knew them so intimately. A random sentence selected from page 25 of the introduction may serve as an example of his descriptive style and powers of observation: "The Romanesque ornaments are very skilfully and delicately drawn, and the old patterns are enlivened by the introduction of a new and variegated foliage, of which the bell-shaped flowers are especially conspicuous." (This comment refers to the Icelandic manuscript AM. 350, fol., the *Skarðsbók*.)

As distant as the subject is in time, Halldór makes the illustrations in medieval manuscripts come alive, in many cases by explaining how they depict some events from daily life in the Middle Ages. His observations are sometimes not without humor, as for example, the remark on page 20: "One cannot expect men to look their best after having been salted and buried, even though they were resurrected by a great saint."

In a review of this volume, Sigurður Nordal, professor of Icelandic literature at the University of Iceland, wrote in the Icelandic periodical *Skírnir* in 1935 that it was an unmitigated pleasure to examine the book and that through it one could see how Icelanders had been able to produce beautiful manuscripts in their own bailiwick. Moreover, on the basis of the illuminations reproduced, one could, he noted, also draw conclusions about the beginnings of Icelandic art.

While Halldór Hermannsson could only applaud the concept of issuing Old Icelandic manuscripts in facsimile and admire the initiative of Ejnar Munksgaard, who was both publisher and general editor of the series *Corpus codicum Islandicorum medii aevi*, he privately stated that the facsimiles were issued in an ill-chosen manner, for the volumes consist of leaves of thin cardboard rather than paper and consequently are heavy and bulky to use. Incidentally, the volumes in the series were given an impressive half-vellum binding imprinted with the coat of arms of Iceland—presumably so that the appearance of the books would attract prospective purchasers; for the time they were priced high. Since Munksgaard apparently was able to amortize his investment in this unusual venture, which could only further Icelandic studies, it was inappropriate to complain openly about the nature of paper and binding.

A direct outgrowth of Halldór's work with illuminated manuscripts of the Middle Ages which had resulted in the folio in the series *Corpus codicum Islandicorum medii aevi* was volume XXVIII of *Islandica* (1940) entitled *Illuminated Manuscripts of the Jónsbók*. The subject attracted him for several reasons. In the first place, the *Jónsbók* is an important collection of laws. In the second, it is preserved in very many—some two hundred—parchment and later paper codices. In the third, it enabled him to extend his treatment of the *Jónsbók* beyond what had been possible in the general work on illuminated manuscripts. In his essay on Icelandic manuscripts (*Islandica* XIX, 1929), Halldór Hermannsson had already reproduced sample pages from the *Jónsbók*, along with sample pages from the *Elder Edda*, the *Flateyjarbók*, and the collection of laws known as *Grágás*.

The introduction to *Islandica* XXVIII repeats some of the information that had appeared in the introduction to the folio volume five years earlier. Thirty plates provide documentary evidence about the art of illumination over a long period of time and additional pictorial representation of life in Iceland, as well as some of the symbolic imagery used throughout Europe through the seventeenth century. In particular, Halldór stresses the use of Romanesque devices in the seventeenth century.

With *Illuminated Manuscripts of the Jónsbók*, Halldór concluded his series of contributions to the study of manuscripts and questions of their preservation and use, except for a statement issued after World War II in his capacity as a member of the Arnamagnaean Commission. In this statement he supported the positive views of Professor Jón Helgason, curator of the Arnamagnaean Collection, regarding the proposed return of manuscripts from Denmark to Iceland.

VII

Historiographic Perspective

Halldór Hermannsson made several contributions into the more traditional fields subsumed under the heading of Icelandic philology and associated with the terms Edda, saga, and *Sturlungaöld*. In turning his attention to several of the great names of medieval Iceland, he maintained the point of view and method of an historian. His effort was to interpret the past and to understand some figures who were themselves historiographically important. He was willing to make conjectures but only upon a factual basis and only if they seemed reasonable.

On the occasion of the one thousandth anniversary of the Icelandic Althing in 1930, Halldór edited and translated the earliest monument of Icelandic history, the so-called *Íslendingabók* by Ari Þorgilsson, and supplied a forty-six-page introductory essay as well as fifteen pages of notes on Ari's text (*Islandica* XX). This is the first of three works that Halldór devoted to subjects taken from preclassical, classical, and post classical Old Norse–Icelandic literature respectively. Like other historians before him and after him, Halldór was impressed by the clarity and quality of Ari's writing and, above all, by Ari's references to his sources, notably to those individuals who, by virtue of their genealogy, could be presumed to transmit accurate information about events that took place one hundred or more years prior to the composition of the *Íslendingabók* around the year 1123. Halldór was much taken with the figure of Ari and wrote what must be called an exhaustive article on him (considering the small amount of information available about him) for the Icelandic annual *Skírnir* in 1948. Halldór's introduction to *Íslendingabók* includes information about the early settlement of Iceland, and discusses the as yet unanswered question about the exact ethnic background of the Icelanders.

Halldór argues convincingly that the *Íslendingabók* cannot have been written before 1122 or after 1125. He also discusses the possible relationship of Ari with the *Landnámabók*, and inclines to the theory that Ari may have been its author, a matter he was to return to in his preface to *Islandica* XXXI, *The Saga of Thorgils and Haflidi*, in 1945.

Despite the brevity of the *Íslendingabók*—and it consists of only a dozen pages in Halldór Hermannsson's edition—we are persuaded in Halldór's introduction that Ari is indeed "one of those personages of the past to whom we confidently look for information and guidance," since Ari's book, as Halldór puts it, "evidences a sincere search for truth and assiduous efforts to secure it" (p. 46). Halldór's translation is straightforward and accurate; only here and there might one have chosen a word less unusual or less archaic. This is not meant to suggest that Halldór's translation in any way contained the infelicitous archaisms of William Morris and his imitators, for Halldór agreed with other twentieth-century critics that Morris and company sorely misrepresented the sagas.

In attempting to reconstruct the life of Sæmund Sigfússon in volume XXII of *Islandica* (1932), Halldór was concerned with a name in the history of Icelandic literature familiar to everyone at all interested in that literature, for in the seventeenth century it had been assumed that Sæmund was the eleventh-to-twelfth-century author of that collection now known as the *Elder Edda*, but formerly referred to as *Sæmundar Edda*. The ascription to Sæmund speaks for the prestige he enjoyed both in his own day and later, and it is therefore natural to ask in what his significance lies. Halldór describes first—on the basis of the skimpy evidence—the importance of Sæmund Sigfússon in his own time, and second—drawing upon more abundant source material—the role his family played in the history of Iceland. The family lived at Oddi and it members were therefore identified as Oddaverjar—which explains Halldór's title: *Sæmund Sigfússon and the Oddaverjar*.

We know that Sæmund was born in 1056 and was the first Icelander to study in France—long before the establishment of the first French university—and that he was persuaded to return to his native land by Jón, the first bishop of Hólar. As priest of the church at Oddi, Sæmund was one of the most influential clergymen in the country if only because his was one of the wealthiest churches. Sæmund was known as "the learned"—*inn fróði*—during his lifetime, but on what basis this cognomen was bestowed is a matter of conjecture. Halldór points out that Ari Þorgilsson submitted his *Íslendingabók* to Sæmund for criticism. Since Ari himself was a learned man, a clear thinker, and an historian, his respect for Sæmund's opinion is not unimportant—and this may be the reason that Halldór's attention was drawn particularly to Sæmund as a subject for historical and genealogical investigation. Halldór finds it probable that Sæmund was the first writer of history in Iceland, although he assumes that Sæmund must have written in Latin. That Snorri Sturluson, who was brought up at Oddi, does not mention Sæmund's name leads Halldór to the conclusion that Snorri "found other and fuller sources for his history than the work left by Sæmund" (p. 35). In discussing the possible relationship between Sæmund and Snorri with regard to the (younger) *Edda*, Halldór inclines to the hypothesis that the term "Edda" may be derived from Oddi and mean the "book of Oddi." The attempt to derive "Edda" from the noun *óðr* meaning "poetry" Halldór finds to be "philological pedantry" (p. 38).

Halldór indicates that relations were friendly between Snorri and the Oddi family and therefore feels it safe to assume that Snorri must have found much of the material he used in the (younger) *Edda* at Oddi. Thus, indirectly, there may have been some connection between Sæmund and Snorri, especially since most scholars agree that Snorri must have worked in part from earlier manuscripts.

Halldór concludes his discussion of Sæmund by describing the role that he plays in some Icelandic folk tales, in which he is sometimes associated with the devil. Halldór propounds the theory that Sæmund's interest in heathen legend and pagan gods might have been looked upon as reprehensible in his own day and that for this reason Sæmund became connected in the popular mind with the powers of evil.

In addition to bringing together what is known about Sæmund Sigfússon and establishing various hypotheses about his activities and historical and literary production, Halldór devotes several pages to the lives of Sæmund's children, grandchildren, and great-grandchildren insofar as such information can be located or deduced from various Icelandic sagas, particularly the *Sturlunga saga* and the *Biskupa sögur*. Halldór takes the story of the Oddaverjar down to the end of the thirteenth century, when the family was no longer identifiable as a unit.

In 1945, finally, Halldór Hermannsson published *The Saga of Thorgils and Haflidi* as volume XXXI of *Islandica*. He elected to print the text of this saga because it is of particular interest as an example of a narrative from the post-saga era, the so-called Age of the Sturlungs: *Sturlungaöld*. It contains descriptions of certain events which seem to be derived from firsthand impressions; the best-known descriptions are of a wedding feast at Reykhólar in the summer of 1119 and of the meetings of the Althing in the years 1120 and 1121. As a consequence, *Þorgils saga ok Hafliða* must be considered historical, in contrast to the traditional heroic sagas, although, as Halldór points out in his introduction, *Þorgils saga* is 'written in the same style as the traditional heroic sagas," with a story similar to that of many of those sagas—basically a quarrel between two chieftains (p. xxvi). As was his wont, Halldór provided explanatory notes identifying people and places that appear in the saga and elucidating words and phrases that would not be readily understood.

The introduction to *The Saga of Thorgils and Haflidi* concerns itself only in part with the saga. After a number of observations about Icelandic history, Halldór proposes that the *Landnámabók* must have been the work of Ari Þorgilsson, known to us as the author of the *Íslendingabók*. Halldór had brought up this idea in his edition of the *Íslendingabók* in 1930. Halldór is, to be sure, not the only scholar who has felt that Ari was the author of *Landnámabók*. In arguing for Ari's authorship, he is supporting the earlier convictions of Guðbrandur Vigfússon and Björn M. Ólsen. Halldór stresses the "remarkable topographical knowledge" demonstrated in the *Landnámabók* which could not have been obtained solely from maps and which therefore must have been derived from personal observation; he guesses that Ari could have obtained much of his information from Bishop Gizur of Skálholt in whose service he was; the bishop was well traveled in Iceland. Halldór felt that there was no other Icelander at the time who possessed the clarity of vision or the genius which was Ari's—and that there is no other candidate as a possible author of the *Landnámabók*.

While this is an interesting and important hypothesis, it does not have direct bearing on *Þorgils saga*, but it bespeaks the motivation for Halldór's selection of the saga as a subject for investigation and dissemination.

The publication of *The Saga of Thorgils and Haflidi* in 1945 marked the end not only of Halldór's active interest in historiography, but also of the long series of bibliographies, editions, and monographs he had prepared for publication in the preceding volumes of *Islandica*. At this time he intended to become an historian of Iceland himself. At the behest of the American-Scandinavian Foundation, he undertook to write a history of Iceland for inclusion in a series of the political histories and histories of the literatures of the Scandinavian countries which the Foundation wanted to publish. He started to examine a large amount of primary and secondary material on which such a history could be based, but progressively crippling arthritis made it more and more difficult for him to move and even to write. His scholarly production did not cease completely, but writing a lengthy history of Iceland—by hand, for he neither used a typewriter nor dictated—was no longer possible, although he was to live a dozen more years.

VIII

A Scholar's Postscript

After a hiatus of thirteen years, during which the volumes of *Islandica* were written by other persons than Halldór Hermannsson—a *History of Icelandic Prose Writers: 1800–1940* by Stefán Einarsson, a *History of Icelandic Poets: 1800–1940* by Richard Beck, a translation of *Hrafns saga Sveinbjarnarsonar* by Anne Tjomsland, a translation of Einar Ól. Sveinsson's *Sturlungaöld* (*The Age of the Sturlungs*) by Jóhann S. Hannesson, and supplements to the *Bibliography of the Eddas* and the bibliographies of *The Sagas of Icelanders*, both compiled by Jóhann S. Hannesson—Halldór prepared an edition of an Icelandic schoolbook of the seventeenth century, *The Hólar Cato*, as volume XXXIX of *Islandica*—just fifty years after he had prepared the first volume, which had appeared in 1908. He lived to see the first proofs of the book; sickness and his death on 28 August 1958 prevented him from laying final hand upon the volume, and it was published posthumously. The supplemental editing of the book was done by Jóhann S. Hannesson, at that time the curator of the Fiske Icelandic Collection.

In the history of schooling in Europe, there is scarcely a work that has been used and read more widely than the so-called distichs of Cato—although, of course, the former ascription to the famous Cato—or Cato Major as he is sometimes called—is without foundation. The volume known as the *Hólar Cato* was probably printed in 1620 and exists in three imperfect copies. It is of interest not only as an example of a seventeenth-century schoolbook, but also because it contains Icelandic translations of the distichs. Moreover, it contains, in addition to the *Catonis Disticha*, a so-called Sayings of the Seven Wise Men of Greece and "De civilitate morum" by Johannes Sulpicius—all with Icelandic translations.

Halldór's introduction to *The Hólar Cato* constitutes an abbreviated history of education in Iceland and in particular at Hólar, with special reference to our knowledge of books that were used in the schools, that is, from the eleventh century onward, for there is documentary evidence of the existence of at least three schools in the eleventh century. Halldór found in the inventory of the Viðey Cloister from 1397, for example, the *Disticha Catonis* listed along with other works he was able to identify with fair certainty. Halldór points out that the schools established according to the Danish church ordinance of the year 1537 were meant in the first instance to teach Latin. Since later ordinances establishing schools in Iceland in the 1540's and 1550's do not go into the matter of instruction, Halldór assumes that the "studies were to be carried on according to the directions given in the church ordinance of 1537" (p. xix). According to that ordinance, two of the first books the pupils were to read were Cato's distichs and the Donatus. The further reading was entirely in Latin until the fifth year, when instruction in Greek might be given. We learn that this situation obtained until 1743, when the place of the native tongue in instruction was recognized. These remarks about the early history of Icelandic schools were especially appropriate, since Halldór's plan to edit the *Hólar Cato* had been generated by the centenary, in 1946, of the Latin school—

then called Menntaskóli—in Reykjavik, from which Halldór had graduated with distinction in 1898.

Because the *Hólar Cato* is a fusion of classical Mediterranean and native Icelandic traditions with both of which Halldór was intimately acquainted, the volume can be called a felicitous memorial to Halldór Hermannsson. In a review of the *Hólar Cato* in *Scandinavian Studies* in 1959 this writer observed that the catholicity and supernational quality of his spirit is again reflected in his final, posthumous contribution to *Islandica*. Moreover, to strike a more personal note, we may infer that the tranquil, stoic, and pragmatic philosophy of Cato Minor, with its aloofness to the metaphysical and its pervasive honesty, represents a not wholly inadequate formulation of the convictions and principles by which Halldór Hermannsson lived.

It is singularly fitting that the *Hólar Cato* was the last volume Halldór compiled, for it provides as much as any other single work a connecting link with Halldór's earliest years as a publishing scholar. The sixth number of Willard Fiske's *Bibliographical Notices* (which constituted the fourth supplement to the British Museum's catalogue on books printed in Iceland) was published in Ithaca, edited and completed by Halldór Hermannsson in 1907. Pages 8 to 12 of this publication include a description of the Icelandic schoolbook containing the *Catonis Disticha*—the *Hólar Cato*. The item had of course been listed peremptorily in the first volume of the catalogue of the Collection in 1914, and had been recorded in Halldór's *Icelandic Books of the Seventeenth Century* in 1922 (*Islandica* XIV).

IX

Professor Hermannsson of Cornell

In the register of Cornell University for 1905/6, published in January 1906, the name of Halldór Hermannsson appears as "instructor in Scandinavian languages." Cornell, where regular instruction in Scandinavian had begun as early as 1864—approximately contemporaneously with the start of such instruction at the University of Wisconsin—once more became one of the few institutions in the United States where it was possible to study the Scandinavian languages and literatures. Cornell was the only American university where the emphasis was clearly upon Icelandic. In his first academic year of teaching, Halldór is listed as offering two courses, one in modern Danish and one in Old Norse, the former taught in the first term, and latter in the second. Danish was described as "a course in the modern literature of the north of Europe. With recitations and lectures." The description does not suggest instruction merely in the Danish language. More surprising, Old Norse was identified as a continuation of the course in modern Danish and was described as being given "for graduate and advanced students of the Germanic languages." Apparently these courses were offered for students who were already well grounded in German and possibly had considerable knowledge of Germanic philology. Otherwise it is difficult to understand how

Professor Hermannsson in 1936

students could have pursued both Danish and Old Norse in the course of one year with profit. The identical courses appear in the catalogue for the following year, but in 1907/8 Halldór was offering his course in Old Norse–Icelandic as "elementary Old Norse" for the first half year, followed by "lectures on Old Norse literature, institutions, religion, family life, and art" for the second half year. This second course, illustrated by lantern slides, was, in the words of the register, "open to all students, but of special interest to students of literature and history." By the fall of 1908 the Old Norse course was identified as elementary Old Icelandic for graduates and "all advanced students of the Germanic languages." There were to be both recitations and lectures, the lectures accompanied by some lantern slides illustrating northern scenery, life, and art. In addition, the course in Danish was now identified as a language course, but given only in the second half year, three times a week.

A general publication about the university and particularly about the College of Arts and Sciences, published in May of 1907, explains that "courses in Old Norse, Danish, and modern Icelandic are given by a native Icelander who studied at Skandinavian [sic] universities." It adds that "the Cornell University Library is fortunate in possessing a unique collection of books on Icelandic literature, a bequest of the late Willard Fiske" (p. 21). By 1909, A. Leroy Andrews had joined the Department of German at the university and it was he who now offered elementary Old Icelandic, but with the identical description of the course when given by Halldór Hermannsson. It may seem strange that Andrews rather than the native-born Icelander gave the course in Old Icelandic, but Andrews was an established scholar in the field and possessed a philological background superior to that of Halldór, who, after all, had studied law at the

University of Copenhagen and whose training was bibliographic rather than linguistic. As a matter of fact, Halldór had resigned his instructorship in Scandinavian languages in 1908, presumably because arrangements were being made for Professor Andrews to teach the Scandinavian courses. By 1910, Andrews was also offering the course in modern Danish. And it was not until the year 1920 that Halldór Hermannsson's name appears again as the regular teacher of Old Icelandic and the modern Scandinavian languages. In 1912, however, a new course was introduced in English on the Viking Age, given by Halldór and meeting only once a week in the second term. It used lantern slides and apparently incorporated part of the material Halldór had originally used in his first Old Norse course. In 1913, Halldór introduced another one-hour-a-week course in English on the Icelandic sagas. The announcement of the College of Arts and Sciences identifies the course as "lectures on the origin, development, characteristics, and historical value of the Icelandic sagas." By this time Halldór had been working with Icelandic sagas, albeit primarily bibliographically, for eight or nine years.

In 1914 a course on Old Norse mythology, also one hour a week, was introduced. It was to alternate with the course on the Viking Age. These courses were not listed by the graduate school of the university in its announcement until 1917, however, since Halldór did not receive an appointment in the Graduate School until November 1916. Halldór's teaching seems to have been minimal at this time, but his salary for teaching was also minimal. His contract for 1919/20 gives his year's salary as fifty dollars for his teaching in the Department of German, the department in which the Scandinavian courses also are listed through the year 1919/20.

In June of 1919, Halldór wrote to Jacob Gould Schurmann, the president of the university, suggesting that the curatorship of the Fiske Icelandic Collection be combined with a teaching position that would be remunerated at the level of an assistant professorship. In his letter he suggested the establishment of a regular sequence of courses including Dano-Norwegian and Swedish in addition to Old Norse–Icelandic and the courses in Old Norse mythology and antiquities already being given. Halldór's initiative led to a reassessment of the position of Scandinavian at Cornell, and in 1920 there was a new departure: A Department of Scandinavian Languages and Literatures was established with Halldór as assistant professor at an annual salary of $1250 (in addition to his salary as curator of $1500). The description in the announcement of the graduate school for 1921/22 (which presumably stemmed from Halldór's pen) read, "The Fiske Icelandic Collection in the University Library comprising about 15,000 books and pamphlets, offers excellent facilities for advanced work in Old Norse–Icelandic language and literature, Norse mythology and heroic legends, runology, and early Scandinavian history, as well as in modern Icelandic language and literature. The library also has a small collection of books on the other modern Scandinavian languages and literatures to which some additions are made annually." The courses which Halldór was prepared to give are listed somewhat summarily merely as "Old Icelandic, History of the Old Norse–Icelandic literature, Norse mythology, Early Scandinavian history, and modern Scandinavian languages and literatures." There is no doubt that some of the tensions engendered by World War I motivated the establishment of a separate Scandinavian department rather than an expansion of the Department of German into a Department of Germanic Languages and Literatures, as happened at numerous other American universities.

The announcement of the College of Arts and Sciences for 1920/21 consequently lists for the first time a complete program in Scandinavian languages and literatures with courses numbered from 1 to 7: Old Icelandic, Danish (and Dano-Norwegian), Swedish, Old Norse mythology, Old Norse–Icelandic literature, modern Scandinavian literatures, and Scandinavian history. All were taught by Halldór Hermannsson. Basically, this series of courses was kept through the remainder of Professor Hermannsson's tenure at the university. The last time a regular program of courses in the Scandinavian languages and literatures appears in the announcement of the College of Arts and Sciences is in 1945/46, when six of the same seven courses that had been listed in 1920 are to be found. The course on mythology was dropped in 1931. In 1920/21 the seventh course is entitled "Early Scandinavian civilization and history." The Old Icelandic course was offered every year, whereas Danish alternated with Swedish, Old Norse mythology alternated with Old Icelandic literature, and modern Scandinavian literature alternated with Scandinavian history. Modern Icelandic was not introduced into the catalogue until 1932. It probably was possible at all times to take special reading courses with Halldór Hermannsson; that situation obtained in the 1930's in any case. The announcement of the college states in 1934, for example, that "the major requirements in certain subjects may be satisfied in part by informal study" in which the work would be "supervised by the major advisor or by a member of the instructing staff." Since Halldór comprised a one-man department, any informal study was with him. Although the description of the Department of Scandinavian Languages and Literatures optimistically lists the courses required for a major in Scandinavian languages and literatures, there were, in fact, no undergraduate majors in the department until 1938, when this writer took his degree in Scandinavian (as well as in German). There was subsequently only one other undergraduate major, Ward H. Goodenough, Cornell 1941. The requirements for a major had not been brought up-to-date for many years, so that an endeavor to fulfill the requirements as stipulated by the announcement of the college in 1937 brought to light the fact that many of the courses in other departments from which hours were to be selected no longer existed, and a new set of rules had to be made *ad hoc*. In the announcement of the college for 1940/41 printed in December of 1939, this situation is reflected and the description for a major in Scandinavian was finally changed and simplified. The Scandinavian courses now remained on the books unaltered until Halldór's retirement.

Although the courses were offered regularly, they did not always attract students; nor was Halldór particularly eager to have students unless they were seriously interested in what he had to offer them. He made no effort to make his courses better known or to encourage students to take them. He was not especially visible during registration periods—perhaps to avoid being bothered by idle inquiry. Anyone who took the trouble to seek him out and express interest in taking a course, however, was welcomed, and the course, whether for one student or several students, was given. The course that had the smallest overall registration was, understandably, modern Icelandic.

The courses that Halldór gave were very different from one another. While Old Icelandic was listed as Scandinavian 1, it was by far the most difficult course, although it was considered basic for completing an (hypothetical) undergraduate major in Scandinavian. It was listed in 1920/21 as being taught only two hours a week throughout the year, but in the next year it was transmuted into a course meeting three hours weekly throughout the year. On occasions, when Professor Hermannsson was on leave, it was taught only one semester of the academic year. As still most often is the case in teaching Old Icelandic at American universities, the first semester was devoted to an acquisition of the language from E. V. Gordon's *Introduction to Old Norse*. In the second semester some sagas and possibly some selections from the *Elder Edda* were read. The method of instruction harked back to nineteenth-century philological tradition, however. The language was studied more or less theoretically at first, with emphasis on the learning of paradigms. Questions were put by Halldór about the phonology and structure of the language before the students were able to read texts. The classwork consisted in translating rather mechanically from Icelandic to English. Halldór then asked about specific forms that appeared in the text. There was, however, little discussion of the material being read, its style, or the ideas that informed it. This time-honored and dull pedagogical method contrasted sharply with Halldór's personality as one knew it outside the classroom, where he was a brilliant raconteur and could discuss Old Icelandic literature—among other subjects–entertainingly. It did not occur to him to be entertaining in the classroom. The courses in modern Scandinavian languages also followed the traditional method of translating from a prepared text. The reading material was selected somewhat haphazardly on the basis of whatever books were available in a number of copies corresponding to the number of students in the class. Thus, in the Danish course during 1937/38, the first book read was the nineteenth-century Danish dramatist Jens Christian Hostrup's play *Eventyr paa Fodrejsen*; it was followed by a volume of the memoirs of Henrik Pontoppidan. The second book proved to be an excellent text—but it was chosen for the same reason as the old-fashioned Hostrup text: it was available in the seven or eight copies that were needed for the class.

The two courses on Old Norse–Icelandic literature in translation, both one semester in duration and meeting two hours a week, were probably considered easy, since they were purely lecture courses with no discussion on the part of the students. A single term paper was required, and there was a final examination. Whereas enrollment in Old Icelandic and the other language courses was consistently small, the enrollment in the literature courses was relatively large. Halldór Hermannsson must have had some inkling that these courses were considered easy: at the first meeting of a large class in the spring of 1936, for example, he looked at the many unfamiliar faces and asked with a trace of slyness, "All of you interested in Scandinavian literature?"

The course in modern Scandinavian literature was not particularly modern. It dealt chiefly with the dramas of Henrik Ibsen with some mention of Bjørnstjerne Bjørnson but only passing reference to the work of August Strindberg. The content of this course probably did not vary from one year to the next. Halldór saw no need to treat Scandinavian literature after World War I. The course in Old Norse–Icelandic literature discussed the *Elder Edda*, *Snorra Edda*, skaldic poetry, and the sagas, but the emphasis was on the sagas since the students could be expected to read from them in translation.

For the years 1905/9, Halldór is identified as an instructor in Scandinavian languages and the amanuensis of the Fiske Icelandic Collection. He subsequently was given the title of lecturer, which he held until 1920, when he became an assistant professor. In 1924 he was promoted to professor—without having held the intermediate rank of associate professor—presumably because of Danish and Icelandic efforts to lure him back to Scandinavia.

In the histories of Cornell University one seeks in vain for some depiction of Halldór Hermannsson, his position within the university, or his vast production. As a bibliographer and a Scandinavian scholar, he nevertheless enjoyed a worldwide reputation and acquired considerable recognition that came, however, almost entirely from Scandinavia. He was decorated three times by the king of Denmark and Iceland on the recommendation of the Icelandic government. He was an honorary member of the Icelandic Literary Society. In 1930 he was given an honorary degree by the University of Iceland. From 1935 to 1952 he was a member of the Arnamagnaean Commission in Copenhagen. He was asked to edit two volumes in the prestigious series *Corpus codicum Islandicorum medii aevi.* Every scholar in Scandinavia knew his work, which is represented in all the scholarly libraries in the world which have any pretensions in the field of Scandinavian language or literature. His labors had not gone unrecognized in the United States, however, for in 1946 he was elected a vice-president of the Modern Language Association of America. Cornell University took cognizance of his eminence by asking him to represent the university at the centenary of the Royal Technological College in Copenhagen in August 1929 and at the three hundredth anniversary of the University of Amsterdam in June 1932.

Nevertheless, at Cornell University Halldór Hermannsson led a rather quiet but dignified existence. As one of the university's most productive scholars, he necessarily spent much time among books in the library and at home. There is no evidence that Halldór Hermannsson was active in making administrative decisions at the university or in the committee work that, probably to a greater extent now than in his day, plagues academe. He was highly respected by those colleagues who knew him well—and it is the more wonder that Morris Bishop did not write about Halldór in his history of Cornell, for Bishop, although considerably younger than Halldór, knew him and held him in high esteem. Moreover, in some of his own addresses from time to time, Bishop called attention to the Fiske Icelandic Collection and the remarkable quality and quantity of Icelandic literature.

Halldór knew all the famous persons associated with the history of Cornell in the first four decades of the twentieth century, at a time when the faculty was smaller and more closely knit than it is today. While he met people easily and spoke readily and entertainingly on many subjects, he was not gregarious and did not go out of his way to seek out new acquaintances or to expand his social life in the academic community. He commented more than once on a feeling of isolation in Ithaca because it was so far from a large urban center and was not readily accessible by public transportation.

Professor Hermannsson was not an unfamiliar figure on campus in the 1930's. Even then he walked with a measured gait, and he had apparently always carried a cane; he did not resemble the usual American academic. His orientation was an international one, also within academe. He carried on an extensive correspondence with various scholars in the United States and in Europe but little of this could be called personal in nature, even though some of his correspondents were his friends.

He was for many years a member of the Publications Board of the American-Scandinavian Foundation and he also served as a trustee of the foundation from 1943 until his death. These duties apparently were welcome to him since they occasioned frequent trips to New York City.

When abroad, Halldór bought extensively, although somewhat eclectically, for the University Library. At all times he was conscious of the lacunae in the Icelandic Collection and closely followed catalogues of bookdealers in which books in Icelandic or about Iceland might be found to add to the collection. He was not merely an agent for the Fiske Collection but a bookman in his own right and a *habitué* of bookstores, notably in London and Copenhagen. He was naturally most interested in items that could be acquired to augment the Fiske Collection and the Cornell University Library as well as his personal library. The large number of business letters preserved in the Fiske Icelandic Collection, while not interesting reading, attest continual communication with booksellers in Reykjavik, Copenhagen, London, and various other places. Halldór had, moreover, many friends among librarians. Some of the friendships, and notably with Sigfús Blöndal, dated back to the first years of the twentieth century. He was a welcome guest in many libraries, particularly the University Library and Royal Library in Copenhagen. He was quite familiar with the maze of catalogues in the Royal Library—perhaps in part because he had been an employee there—and he enjoyed the unusual privilege of access to the stacks of that library.

Halldór Hermannsson came to interest himself in every aspect of a book—to be sure in the first instance in its content, but to no small degree also in its appearance: typeface, layout, illustration, the quality of the printing, the nature of the paper, and the workmanship of the binding. Several of his own publications attest a keen interest in illustrations and bindings. His article on "Book Illustration in Iceland" took up the first twenty pages of the volume of *Bibliographical Notes*, which constituted volume XXIX of *Islandica* in 1942. When Jóhann S. Hannesson visited Halldór on his deathbed in August of 1958, Halldór stared at the ceiling of his hospital room and said with fervor, "Isn't that a beautiful binding!" A bibliophile he remained to the end, even in the world of hallucination. Halldór pursued several lesser hobbies, some of which were notably bookish. In the course of years he had acquired a collection of the works of James Thomson in various languages, and he also had a large collection of Horace. These collections he sold several years before his death, through the Dauber and Pine Bookstore in New York.

After coming to Cornell in 1905, much of Halldór's time was spent in organizing the Icelandic Collection, cataloguing the books, and subsequently preparing the manuscript of the first volume of the printed catalogue of the collection. Concurrently the collection grew rather rapidly from 8,000 books in 1905 to 23,000 books in 1942. Until his last years, all the work in the collection was performed by Halldór himself. It is impossible to assess how many hours it must have taken to classify and catalogue the thousands of books acquired by the collection during the forty years in which he served as its curator. The preparation of the first volume of the catalogue (published in 1914) was a Herculean task that he performed without help from anyone. Not only are the individual books listed with pertinent bibliographical information and not infrequently with some brief critical comment, but at the end of the volume is found an extensive subject index. The method of preparation for the second and third volumes of the catalogue of the collection was identical. Volume II appeared in 1927 and volume III in 1943. The exacting nature of the proofreading required in preparing volumes I and II for publication was experienced by this writer in the summer of 1942 when employed for a short time as Halldór Hermannsson's research assistant to read proof on volume III of the catalogue of the collection. Incidentally, the classification system used on the books in the collection was developed expressly for the collection, presumably by drawing in part upon Halldór's experience at the Royal Library in Copenhagen.

Halldór was always ready to welcome guests visiting the Fiske Icelandic Collection. The visitors fell into two general categories: Icelanders who merely wanted to see the collection and call upon a fellow countryman, and scholars from other parts of the world who wanted to make use of the collection and to draw upon its curator's fund of bibliographical and historical knowledge. There were, of course, patrons from within the university, students and colleagues, but their number was rather small. Halldór was never too busy to converse with his visitors and help them with any problem they might bring to him. He did not give up the search for information easily, whether the information was sought by others or by himself. Since he was a superb bibliographer, he was familiar with an infinite number of reference works and periodicals in several languages, and ferreted out what he sought quietly and efficiently. In turn, Halldór invariably asked his visitors for news—of the outside world, of Iceland, of places where they had been, of mutual acquaintances, and of world events. He was insatiable in acquiring new information and assimilating new facts, as well as keeping up on the activities of his friends and acquaintances. He conversed easily in both Icelandic and English. His command of English was excellent; only here and there did some unidiomatic phrase betray his origin. Thus, he regularly asked visitors, "What are the news?" No one had the heart to correct this simple error in English idiom in the speech of a dignified gentleman of the old school.

It is not an exaggeration to say that Halldór Hermannsson probably never felt completely acclimatized in the United States; he retained his Icelandic citizenship until his death. While he was equally at home in Ithaca or New York or London or Copenhagen or Reykjavik, he was not so much an internationalist or cosmopolitan that he lost sight of his national origins or put his interest in other countries above his interest in Iceland. He followed the Icelandic press as faithfully as the *New York Times* and was ever able and ready to answer questions informatively regarding the current state of affairs in Iceland.

He was a good correspondent and never one to let an exchange of letters lapse. Sigurður Nordal and Sir William Craigie were among the best known scholars with whom he corresponded frequently, but the number of his other correspondents is legion; they all had some association with or interest in Iceland. None of the letter writing was casual or idle. There is an undertone in all his letters of scholarly endeavor—and an ironic attitude toward opportunism and political extremes. Of his private life, his religiophilosophical persuasion, his early love of outdoor life, his social activities, or even his appreciation of British humor (especially in *Punch*), his letters provide almost no evidence. At least in his later years, he experienced loneliness. He did admit regret that he never married.

X

A Retrospect

Viewing Halldór Hermannsson's life and work in a larger context, one recognizes in him a member of the republic of letters and a champion of learning from whose work both his contemporaries and the succeeding generation have benefited immeasurably. His scholarly endeavors were no more confined to the Cornell University campus than was his own intellectual orientation. He cannot be said to have been a big fish in a small pond: many of his colleagues at Cornell University and probably most students at the university knew next to nothing of his work; but this was apparently a matter of no consequence to him. Moreover, despite his concentration on matters Icelandic, he was a man of broad erudition; his intellectual curiosity drove him to the acquisition of encyclopedic knowledge. In the spirit of a devotee of the Enlightenment, he was dedicated to the search for knowledge and the ordering of information. His perseverance and *honnête ambition* led him to make a lengthy series of contributions in the form of bibliographies, catalogues, and monographs, all of which added many cubits specifically to our knowledge of Icelandic history and culture. He forged many tools to be passed into the hands of other scholars. For more than half a century the serious study of Old Norse literature and Icelandic history has been unthinkable without the utilization of those tools. His scholarly attitudes and method were not parochial, for he treated Icelandic matters in an international and, more particularly, European context. Working essentially alone, removed a great distance from the subject of his researches and removed also from other scholars both in the United States and in northern Europe who were concerned with similar or related problems, he nevertheless was able to maintain a sovereign position in the realm of scholarship. This fact is evidenced best in his relation to the Arnamagnaean Commission in Copenhagen. It was Halldór Hermannsson who felt and articulated the need for a reform and reorganization of the commission and who was able to make concrete and practical suggestions for effecting that reform. The fact that he was four thousand miles from Copenhagen and the Arnamagnaean Collection did not lessen the impact he had upon the minds of those persons responsible for the continuance and functioning of that collection.

On a different level, Halldór unstintingly disseminated information about Iceland abroad and contributed to the cultural interplay between Iceland and other western nations. Recognized as a font of knowledge and an authority in his field, he received a constant stream of inquiries about Icelandic, Old Norse, and more general Scandinavian matters—from dilettantes as well as scholars, from laymen as well as students. To all of these inquiries he endeavored to supply accurate information and succinct answers.

Singlehandedly, Halldór had turned a bibliophile's treasure house into a center of scholarly activity and productivity. Willard Fiske had not been a dilettante—he had after all taught the Scandinavian languages at Cornell University when he was a professor there—but his interest in Iceland was something of a hobby. In Fiske's later years he spared no effort or expense in gathering as much printed documentary evidence as possible, but the creation of a comprehensive collection per se and not its exploitation was his major goal. Halldór did not underestimate the value of keeping up a comprehensive collection of material in a certain field, but he was not satisfied simply with the continued expansion of the collection. He wanted both to make its contents accessible to researchers and to make use of it himself to the best of his abilities in order to help push back the borders of the unknown on one front or the other.

This did not mean, however, that he failed to recognize Willard Fiske's achievement or give him his just due. Writing in the short-lived monthly periodical *Scandinavia* in 1924 (No. 6, p. 12) he remarked, "The Fiske Icelandic Collection is the work of a scholar and a book collector in one person. The scholar brought there together all the printed works which are necessary for any serious student of the subject, but many items are to be found there which have been gathered by the collector who loved to hunt a rare book or a fugitive pamphlet for the pleasure of which, first, the chase gave him and, afterwards, the possession of it. This is a happy combination in any founder of a library."

From the first, Halldór realized that utilization of the collection depended on making its contents known. This need was met between 1914 and 1943 by the publication of three catalogues of the collection. The specialized bibliographies that began publication even before the catalogues methodically organized a large amount of information that could be drawn upon for further study. These specialized bibliographies listed not only books by subject but also articles and reviews and thus enabled a user to orient himself on the scholarly work done on any given subject up to the publication of a particular bibliography. To be sure, almost all of the material recorded in the bibliographical volumes of *Islandica* is to be found in the Fiske Icelandic Collection, but the listing under the proper heading of articles and reviews published in journals bespeaks perspicacity and persistence on the part of a dedicated bibliographer who understood the subject matter he was recording.

In retrospect one observes five major interests represented in Halldór Hermannsson's publications: the first is the bibliography of medieval literature, that is, the sagas, the *Eddas*, and old Icelandic law; the second, the problem of the Scandinavian discovery and settlement of the North American continent; the third, the literature of the sixteenth and seventeenth centuries—something that had attracted little attention hitherto, even among Scandinavian scholars; the fourth, the fate of Icelandic literature in the world and outside interest in Icelandic literature and language; the fifth, the illustration of manuscripts and books. Most of his works can be classified under these rubrics, although no small number of lesser items falls outside of them. While these categories represent the major currents of Halldór's scholarly activity and thought, there was a constant undercurrent that deserves mention: a patriotic concern with the preservation of indigenous Icelandic language and culture and, consciously or unconsciously, support for the idea of Icelandic political independence, despite his conviction that Iceland should remain within the Scandinavian political as well as cultural sphere.

All of Halldór's publications were well researched and were worked out with both erudition and care, as can be observed merely by glancing at the learned footnotes and contemplating the vast literature in several languages to which these footnotes refer. It was an essential trait of Halldór Hermannsson to familiarize himself thoroughly with any topic that had a bearing or even was tangential to the subject on which he was working. Moreover, any subject that could be connected directly with Iceland was of interest to him. An anecdote from the year 1938 is perhaps not out of place: A student heard Halldór discourse with considerable authority on the volcanoes of Arabia and was at a loss to understand the source or reason for his knowledge of that apparently esoteric subject. Puzzled, he asked Professor Hermannsson, "How can it be that you know so much about volcanoes in Arabia?" The question seemed to surprise Professor Hermannsson, who answered in a straightforward but naive fashion, "There are volcanoes in Iceland." To him that was sufficient explanation and also sufficient reason for his familiarizing himself in this instance with the history of volcanoes in various parts of the world.

Willard Fiske made scarcely any greater contribution to scholarship than his selection of Halldór Hermannsson, first, as his assistant in setting up the Icelandic collection when it was still in Florence and, second, in suggesting that Halldór Hermannsson be made the first curator of the collection in Ithaca. By fortuitous circumstance Fiske had selected the right man to make the best use of his Icelandic books, if it was his ambition to create a living monument to himself and to achieve immortality by means of the printed word. Through the printed catalogues in particular, those who could not come to Ithaca to use the collection within the context of a large university library could deduce considerable information and also draw upon its riches. They were more fortunate who were able to work in the collection itself. There is no roster of the many scholars who in the course of years have made use of this collection firsthand; but much of the work of Stefán Einarsson, Richard Beck, and Haraldur Bessason was generated in the collection itself, where they worked for longer or shorter periods of time. In particular, the late Stefán Einarsson of Johns Hopkins University spent the summers of many years in Ithaca in order to be near the collection. Other students and research workers were able to visit and use it only now and then or on special occasions, and all such persons can attest the intrinsic value of the collection as well as the invaluable help they received from its curators, first from Halldór and subsequently from his successors. The Fiske Icelandic Collection is simply without equal in the United States. Although holdings in Icelandic have increased in recent years and especially at the library of the University of Manitoba, Halldór's observation in the periodical *Scandinavia* in 1924 (No. 6, p. 13) still has validity: "While there are in this country some fairly good collections of works on the Old-Icelandic language and literature, like the Maurer Collection in the Harvard University Library, and the Riant Collection in the Yale University Library, and perhaps some others, there is none which can compare in size with the Fiske Collection, especially as to modern Icelandic literature and books written in foreign tongues about Iceland and its affairs."

Halldór realized that the future of the Fiske Icelandic Collection could be threatened by various financial exigencies, but doubtless he could take some solace in the fact that the nucleus and substance of the collection were irreplaceable and would continue to be an invaluable source of early Scandinavica for many decades to come. Presumably moved by this consideration, he left a sum of money in his will so that catalogues of the collection to which he had devoted his life could be reprinted after his death.

Of the several sketches of Halldór Hermannsson's life which have appeared in print hitherto, the most detailed is that by Stefán Einarsson in the annual of the National Library of Iceland for 1957–58 (Reykjavik, 1959). Stefán knew Halldór well. At the beginning of his article, he gives a brief genealogy of Halldór Hermannsson. This genealogy includes several distinguished forebears—presumably unavoidable in the case of every Icelander.[1] In any case, Halldór was not given to talking about his forebears. Stefán then speaks briefly of Halldór as a teacher and a scholar, stressing the bibliographical contributions and sketching Halldór's relationship with the Arnamagnaean Collection. The last three pages comprise a kind of personal memoir, centered upon Halldór's last years, which were marred by crippling arthritis. Like all those persons who were privileged to know Halldór Hermannsson, Stefán prized him for his social grace as well as his learning, his abilities as a conversationalist as well as a productive scholar, and his loyalty to his friends as well as to the unending search for truth. "His opinions were strong, his judgments often sharp," observe the authors of the necrology issued by Cornell University in 1959. "Much engaged in controversy, he was always an honorable, though redoubtable opponent." The Cornell necrology—written by Morris Bishop, Professor of French, Jóhann Hannesson, then Curator of the Fiske Icelandic Collection, and Robert M. Ogden, former Dean of the College of Liberal Arts—all of whom had known Halldór Hermannsson well—concludes with the sentence, "He was a fine example of scholarly serenity, of the philosophy, learned from books, which comforts the spirit and defies the augmenting, dissolving pains of the body."

[1] Halldór Hermannsson's genealogy back to the fifteenth century is to be found in Guðbrandur Jónsson's article "Nogle Oplysninger om tre islandske Adelsslægter," *Personalhistorisk Tidsskrift* 6th ser. VI (1915), 35–39.

There is no stone marker upon which the name of Halldór Hermannsson has been chiseled and no bronze plaque to suggest to posterity the life and work of a guardian of humanistic values—nor is there need of stone or bronze: the Icelandic Collection, its catalogues, and the series *Islandica* constitute his monument.

A Bibliography of the Writings of Halldór Hermannsson

Based on a Compilation by Stefán Einarsson

After the death of Halldór Hermannsson in August of 1958, the late Stefán Einarsson undertook to assemble a bibliography of his works to accompany a memorial article printed in the annual of the National Library of Iceland for 1958–59 (*Landsbókasafn Íslands. Árbók*, Reykjavik, 1959; the article and bibliography are found on pages 139–62).

Professor Einarsson's compilation was based on books and articles by Halldór Hermannsson accessible in the Fiske Icelandic Collection and, with respect to reviews, on Halldór's own notations. Professor Einarsson did not have the opportunity to expand the bibliography or to check all notations for completeness.

The present bibliography, which (unlike Stefán Einarsson's) is chronological rather than systematic, proceeds from an examination of all books, articles, and reviews listed. Numerous entries from Professor Einarsson's list have been revised for the sake of accuracy and consistency. Some fifty entries are new.

1897

Articles:

"Abdul Hamid Tyrkjasoldán." *Ísland*, 3 April 1897. (Pseud. Hrærekur.)

"Drúsar. Eftir dr. J. Östrup." *Ísland*, 27 Feb. 1897. (Pseud. Heiðrekur.)

"Dýrin og löggjöfin (eftir Schenkling-Prévôt)." *Ísland*, 28 Aug. 1897. (Pseud. Heiðrekur.)
"Frá Grikklandi." *Ísland*, 17, 24 July 1897. (Pseud. Heiðrekr.)
"Konur og prestar. Eftir C. Lombróso." *Ísland*, 11 Sept. 1897. (Pseud. Hjeðinn.)
"Samningatilraun um sölu Kúbu fyrir 60 árum. (Að mestu eftir Kringsjá)." *Ísland*, 16 Jan. 1897. (Pseud. Hrærekur.)
"Söguvilla. (Eftir R. Vasucleva Ran, þýtt úr 'Kringsjaa')." *Ísland*, 30 Jan. 1897. (Pseud. Heiðrekr.)
"Týndir norðurfarar. (Að nokkru eftir 'Hver 8. Dag')." *Ísland*, 30 Oct. 1897. (Pseud. Hrærekur.)

1898

Articles:

"Aldur mannkynsins eftir Joseph Prestwich." *Ísland*, 7 June 1898. (Pseud. Heiðrekur.)
"Frá útlöndum." *Ísland*, 15 Oct. 1898. (Anon.) [Letter dtd. Copenhagen 25 Sept.]
"Frá útlöndum." *Ísland*, 24 Oct. 1898 (Anon.) [Letter dtd. Copenhagen 27 Sept.]
"Frá útlöndum." *Ísland*, 8 Nov. 1898. (Anon.) [Letter dtd. Copenhagen 12 Oct.]
"Frá útlöndum." *Ísland*, 22 Nov. 1898. (Anon.) [Letter dtd. Copenhagen 12 Oct.]
"Frá útlöndum." *Ísland*, 29 Nov. 1898. (Anon.) [Letter dtd. Copenhagen 14 Nov.]
"Makedónia og austræna málið." *Ísland*, 14 June 1898. (Pseud. Heiðrekur.) [Translated from Danish version of article by Spiridoa Gopocevic.]

1899

Articles:

"Frá útlöndum." *Ísland*, 31 Jan. 1899. (Anon.) [Letter dtd. Copenhagen 14 Jan.]

"Frá útlöndum." *Ísland*, 13 April 1899. (Anon.) [Letter dtd. Copenhagen 4 April.]
"Frá útlöndum." *Ísland*, 14 May 1899. (Anon.) [Letter dtd. Copenhagen 24 April.]
"Um Íslendinga í 'København.'" *Ísland*, 31 Jan. 1899. (Pseud. "X") [Letter dtd. Copenhagen 14. Jan.]

1901

Article:

"Skákbókasafn." *Þjóðólfur*, 20 Sept. 1901. (Pseud. "X.")

1901–1902

Periodical:

Í uppnámi: Íslenzkt skákrit. Gefið út fyrir Taflfélag Reykjavíkur. [Leipzig], 1901–2. Pp. vi, 187; viii, 86. [Vol. I ed. by W. Fiske and Halldór Hermannsson, vol. II by Halldór Hermannsson alone.]

1905

Article:

"Willard Fiske." *Eimreiðin* XI (1905), 104–9.

1907

Book:

Bibliographical Notices VI. Books Printed in Iceland 1578–1844. A Fourth Supplement to the British Museum Catalogue. With a General Index to the Four Supplements. Ithaca, New York, 1907. Pp. 48. [By Willard Fiske; revised and completed by Halldór Hermannsson.]

Reviewed in: *Eimreiðin* XIV (1908), 236, by Valtýr Guðmundsson.
Evening Post (New York), Saturday Supplement, 18 Jan. 1908, by B. S. Monroe.
Lögrjetta, 19 Feb. 1908, by Sigfús Blöndal.
Anzeiger für deutsches Altertum XXXIII (1909), 307–8, by B. Kahle.

Review:

Paul Herrmann, *Island in Vergangenheit und Gegenwart. The Nation* LXXV (1907), 587–88. (Anon.)

1908

Book:

Islandica: An Annual Relating to Iceland and the Fiske Icelandic Collection in Cornell University Library. Edited by George William Harris, Librarian. Volume I. *Bibliography of the Icelandic Sagas and Minor Tales.* Ithaca, New York: Issued by Cornell University Library, 1908. Pp. (14), 126.

Also issued as a separate: *Bibliography of the Icelandic Sagas and Minor Tales.* Ithaca, N.Y.: Printed by Andrus & Church, 1908. Pp. (6), 126.

Reviewed in: *Orkney & Shetland Old-lore* I (1907–8), 332–33.
Deutsche Literaturzeitung XXIX (1908), cols. 3149–50, by B. Kahle.
Lögrjetta, 22 July 1908.
New England Historical and Genealogical Register LXII (1908), 393.
Óðinn IV (1908), 48, by Þorsteinn Gíslason.
Revue critique d'histoire et de littérature, n.s. LXVI (1908), 411–12, by Léon Pineau.
Times Literary Supplement, 16 July 1908, pp. 231–32.
Breiðablik (Winnipeg) III (1908–9), 154, by [Friðrik J. Bergmann].
Literarisches Zentralblatt LX (1909), cols. 510–11, by E. P. Evans.

Literaturblatt für germanische und romanische Philologie XXX (1909), cols. 185–86, by Wolfgang Golther.

Lögrjetta, 27 Feb. 1909, by Sigfús Blöndal.

Studi de filologia moderna II (1909), 164.

Anzeiger für deutsches Altertum XXXIV (1910), 178–80, by Gustav Neckel.

Eimreiðin XVI (1910), 76, by Valtýr Guðmundsson.

Jahresbericht für germanische Philologie XXX (1910), 59–60.

(Svensk) *Historisk tidskrift* XXX (1911), 298–99, by V. Gödel.

Nordisk Tidskrift för Bok- och Biblioteksväsen I (1914), 93–95, by Sigfús Blöndal.

1909

Articles:

"Dufferin lávarður." *Óðinn* V (1909/10), 41–43.

"Fiske-safnið." *Óðinn* IV (1908/9), 73–75.

"Forsetaskiptin í Bandaríkjunum." *Lögrjetta*, 5 May 1909. (Pseud. Sig. Lontano.)

"Fræðsla um Ísland." *Lögrjetta*, 29 Sept. 1909.

"Graft." *Lögrjetta*, 27 Nov. 1909. (Pseud. Peregrinus.)

"Hin nýju tolllög Bandamanna." *Lögrjetta*, 27 Oct. 1909. (Pseud. Sig. Lontano.)

"Upptök styrjalda." *Lögrjetta*, 26 May 1909. (Pseud. Sig. Lontano.)

"Viðskiptaráðanauturinn." *Lögrjetta*, 20 Oct. 1909. (Pseud. Peregrinus.)

"Xavier Marmier." *Óðinn* V (1909/10), 31–34.

Book:

Islandica: An Annual Relating to Iceland and the Fiske Icelandic Collection in Cornell University Library. Edited by George William Harris, Librarian. Volume II. *The Northmen in America*. Ithaca, New York: Issued by Cornell University Library, 1909. Pp. (10), 94.

Also issued as a separate: *The Northmen in America (982–c. 1500): A Contribution to the Bibliography of the Subject*. Ithaca, N.Y.: Printed by Andrus & Church, 1909. Pp. (8), 94.

Reviewed in: *Anzeiger für deutsches Altertum* XXXIII (1909), 308, by Edward Schroeder.

Deutsche Literaturzeitung XXX (1909), cols. 2351–52, by B. Kahle.

Lögrjetta, 3 Nov. 1909, by Sigfús Blöndal.

Dr. A. Petermanns Mitteilungen LVI (1910), 223–24, by Viktor Hantzsch.

Eimreiðin XVI (1910), 76, by Valtýr Guðmundsson.

1910

Articles:

"Ábyrgð blaðanna." *Lögrjetta*, 20 April 1910. (Pseud. Peregrinus.)

"Bannlögin." *Lögrjetta*, 28 Dec. 1910.

"'Bláa bókin' o. fl." *Lögrjetta*, 20 July 1910.

"Gott nafn og ilt." *Lögrjetta*, 26 Jan. 1910. (Pseud. Peregrinus.)

"Quousque tandem—?" *Lögrjetta*, 27 July 1910. (Pseud. Peregrinus.)

"Vín og vínbann." *Eimreiðin* XVI (1910), 187–98.

Book:

Islandica: An Annual Relating to Iceland and the Fiske Icelandic Collection in Cornell University Library. Edited by George William Harris, Librarian. Volume III. *Bibliography of the Sagas of the Kings of Norway and Related Sagas and Tales*. Ithaca, New York: Issued by Cornell University Library, 1910. Pp. (8), 75.

Also issued as a separate: *Bibliography of the Sagas of Kings of Norway and Related Sagas and Tales*. Ithaca, N.Y.: Printed by Andrus & Church, 1910. Pp. (6), 75.

Reviewed in: *Deutsche Literaturzeitung* XXXI (1910), cols. 2702–3, by B. Kahle.

Eimreiðin XVI (1910), 232, by Valtýr Guðmundsson.

Lögrjetta, 6 July 1910, by Sigfús Blöndal.

Folk-Lore XXII (1911), 270–71, by L. W. Faraday.

Lögberg, 25 Jan. 1912.

Anzeiger für deutsches Altertum XXXVII (1914), 50–51, by Gustav Neckel.

Literaturblatt für germanische und romanische Philologie XXXV (1914), cols. 150–51, by August Gebhardt.

1911

Articles:

"Bréf frá Finni biskupi [Jónssyni]." *Eimreiðin* XVII (1911), 134–36.

"Íslenzka bókasafnið í Cornell." *Lögberg*, 21 Dec. 1911.

Book:

Islandica: An Annual Relating to Iceland and the Fiske Icelandic Collection in Cornell University Library. Edited by George William Harris, Librarian. Volume IV. *The Ancient Laws of Norway and Iceland: A Bibliography.* Ithaca, New York: Issued by Cornell University Library, 1911. Pp. (10), 83.

Also issued as a separate: *The Ancient Laws of Norway and Iceland: A Bibliography.* Ithaca, N.Y.: Printed by Andrus & Church, 1911. Pp. (8), 83.

Reviewed in: *Deutsche Literaturzeitung* XXXII (1911), cols. 2953–54, by Karl Lehmann.

Lögrjetta, 25 Oct. 1911, by Sigfús Blöndal.

Eimreiðin XVIII (1912), 156, by Valtýr Guðmundsson.

Lögberg, 25 Jan. 1912.

Literaturblatt für germanische und romanische Philologie XXXV (1914), cols. 150–51, by August Gebhardt.

Review:

Gunnar Castrén, *Norden i den franska litteraturen. The Nation* XCII (1911), 297. (Anon.)

1912

Book:

Islandica: An Annual Relating to Iceland and the Fiske Icelandic Collection in Cornell University Library. Edited by George William Harris,

Librarian. Volume V. *Bibliography of the Mythical-Heroic Sagas.* Ithaca, New York: Issued by Cornell University Library, 1912. Pp. (10), 73.

Also issued as a separate with series title page repeated (by mistake) and added title page: *Bibliography of the Mythical-Heroic Sagas (Fornaldarsögur)*. Ithaca, N.Y.: Printed by Andrus & Church. Pp. (10), 73.

Reviewed in: *Lögrjetta*, 16 Oct. 1912, by Sigfús Blöndal.
Eimreiðin XIX (1913), 151–52, by Valtýr Guðmundsson.
Folk-Lore XXIV (1913), 533, by L. W. Faraday.
Deutsche Literaturzeitung XXXV (1914), cols. 715–17, by August Gebhardt.

Review:

Björn M. Ólsen, ed., *Stúfs saga gefin út í first sinn eftir handritunum.* Reykjavik, 1912. (Supplement to *Árbók Háskóla Íslands* 1911–12.) *Lögberg*, 19 Dec. 1912. [Under heading "Háskóli Íslands."]

1913

Articles:

"Íslenskur málari [Þorsteinn Illugason Hjaltalín]." *Óðinn* IX, (1913/14), 1–2.

"Hið íslenzka fræðafélag í Kaupmannahöfn." *Lögberg*, 5 June 1913.

"J. Pierpont Morgan." *Lögrjetta*, 30 Aug. 1913.

"Klassiskar bókmentir." *Lögrjetta*, 1 Jan. 1913. [On the Loeb Classical Library.]

"Ný merkisbók í vændum. Ferðabók Þorvaldar Thoroddsen." *Lögrjetta*, 26 March 1913. (Pseud. Homo Islandus.)

Book:

Icelandic Authors of To-day. With an Appendix giving a List of Works dealing with Modern Icelandic Literature. Ithaca, N.Y.: Issued by Cornell University Library, 1913. (*Islandica: An Annual Relating to Iceland and the Fiske Icelandic Collection in Cornell*

University Library. Edited by George William Harris, Librarian. Volume VI. Ithaca, New York: Issued by Cornell University Library.) Pp. xiv, 69.

Also issued as a separate: *Icelandic Authors of To-day*. With an Appendix giving a List of Works dealing with Modern Icelandic Literature. Ithaca, N.Y.: Printed by Andrus & Church, 1913. Pp. iii–xiv, 69.

Reviewed in: *The Athenaeum*, 13 Sept. 1913, p. 251.

Berlingske Tidende (Copenhagen), 13 Dec. 1913, by B. Th. Melsteð.

Lögrjetta, 15 Oct. 1913, by Sigfús Blöndal.

The Nation XCVII (1913), 277–78.

Nýtt kirkjublað VIII (1913), 277–78.

Deutsche Literaturzeitung XXXV (1914), cols. 715–17, by August Gebhardt.

Eimreiðin XX (1914), 154–55, by Valtýr Guðmundsson.

Ísafold, 18 Feb. 1914, by Matthías Jochumsson.

Revue critique d'histoire et de littérature, n.s. LXXVII (1914), 77, by Léon Pineau.

Skírnir LXXXVIII (1914), 428–30, by Páll Eggert Ólason.

Mitteilungen der Islandfreunde II (1914/15), 21, by W. Heydenreich.

Publications of the Society for the Advancement of Scandinavian Study II (1914–15), 279–80, by Charles A. Williams.

Archiv für das Studium der neueren Sprachen CXXXIII (1915), 239, by W. R.

Dr. A. Petermanns Mitteilungen LXI (1915), 164, by Th. Thoroddsen.

1914

Books:

Catalogue of the Icelandic Collection Bequeathed by Willard Fiske. Compiled by Halldór Hermannsson. Ithaca, N.Y., 1914. Pp. viii, (4), 755. [At head of title: Cornell University Library.]

Reviewed in: *Archiv für das Studium der neueren Sprachen und Literaturen* CXXXII (1914), 457.
Deutsche Literaturzeitung XXXV (1914), cols. 1416–20, by Paul Herrmann.
Eimreiðin XX (1914), 229, by Valtýr Guðmundsson.
Heimskringla, 21 May 1914.
Skírnir LXXXVIII (1914), 422–28, by Páll Eggert Ólason.
Sunnanfari XIII (1914), 27.
Literarisches Zentralblatt LXVI (1915), cols. 638–39, by August Gebhardt.
Lögrjetta, 17 Feb. 1915, by Sigfús Blöndal.
Modern Language Notes XXX (1915), 23–24, by Lee M. Hollander.
Nordisk Tidskrift för Bok- och Biblioteksväsen II (1915), 178–82, by Sigfús Blöndal.
Nuova antologia, 5th ser. CLXXIX (1915), 158.
Cornell Alumni News XVIII (1915/16), 380. [Partial translation of Sigfús Blöndal's review in *Nordisk Tidskrift för Bok- och Biblioteksväsen*.]
Anzeiger für deutsches Altertum XL (1920/21), 81, by Gustav Neckel.
Analecta Bollandiana XLVII (1929), 182–83, by P. Grosjean.

The Story of Griselda in Iceland. Edited with an Introduction by Halldór Hermannsson. Ithaca, N.Y.: Issued by Cornell University Library, 1914. (*Islandica: An Annual Relating to Iceland and the Fiske Icelandic Collection in Cornell University Library*. Edited by George William Harris, Librarian. Volume VII. Ithaca, New York: Issued by Cornell University Library.) Pp. (6), xviii, 48.

Reviewed in: *Lögrjetta*, 14 Oct. 1914, by Sigfús Blöndal.
Nordisk Tidskrift för Bok- och Biblioteksväsen I (1914), 386–87, by Sigfús Blöndal.
Deutsche Literaturzeitung XXXVI (1915), cols. 708–9, by August Gebhardt.
Eimreiðin XXI (1915), 75–76, by Valtýr Guðmundsson.

Giornale storico della letteratura italiana LXV (1915), 470.
Skírnir XCI (1917), 195–97, by Páll Eggert Ólason.

Review:

Bréf Páls Melsteðs til Jóns Sigurðssonar, gefin út af hinu íslenzka fræðafélagi í Kaupmannahöfn. Lögberg, 26 Feb. 1914. [Under heading "Ritfregn."]

1915

Articles:

"Icelandic Libraries in America." *American-Scandinavian Review* III (1915), 169–73.

"Ísland og útlendir ferðamenn." *Lögrjetta,* 8 Sept. 1915.

"Viðskifti við útlönd á dögum þjóðveldisins." *Lögrjetta,* 18 Aug. 1915. [In part a review of "Ferðir, siglingar og samgöngur milli Íslands og annara landa á dögum þjóðveldisins," *Safn til sögu Íslands* IV.]

Book:

An Icelandic Satire (Lof lýginnar) Written at the Beginning of the Eighteenth Century by Þorleifur Halldórsson. Edited with an Introduction and Appendix by Halldór Hermannsson. Ithaca, N.Y.: Issued by Cornell University Library, 1915. (*Islandica: An Annual Relating to Iceland and the Fiske Icelandic Collection in Cornell University Library.* Volume VIII. *An Icelandic Satire Written at the Beginning of the Eighteenth Century.* Ithaca, New York: Issued by Cornell University Library, 1915.) Pp. (6) xix, (1), 54, (1).

Reviewed in: *Lögberg,* 30 Sept. 1915.
Lögrjetta, 29 Dec. 1915, by Sigfús Blöndal.
American-Scandinavian Review IV (1916), 120.
Eimreiðin XXII (1916), 155, by Valtýr Guðmundsson.
Nordisk Tidskrift för Bok- och Biblioteksväsen III (1916), 74–77, by Sigfús Blöndal.

Skírnir XCI (1917), 197–99, by Páll Eggert Ólason.
Deutsche Literaturzeitung XLI (1920), cols. 687–88, by Gustav Neckel.

Reviews:

Afmælisrit til dr. phil. Kr. Kålunds, bókavarðar við safn Árna Magnússonar. Lögberg, 4 Feb. 1915.

Þorvaldur Thoroddsen, *Ferðabók: Skýrslur um rannsóknir á Íslandi 1882–1898. Lögberg*, 7 Oct. 1915.

1916

Articles:

"Icelandic-American Periodicals." *Publications of the Society for the Advancement of Scandinavian Study* III (1916), 200–212. Reproduced in Icelandic translation in *Lögberg*, 12, 19, 26 Oct. and 2 Nov. 1916, as "Íslenzk tímarit í Vesturheimi."

"Skjaldarmerki Íslands." *Eimreiðin* XXII (1916), 157–75.

Book:

Icelandic Books of the Sixteenth Century (1534–1600). Ithaca, N.Y.: Issued by Cornell University Library, 1916. (*Islandica: An Annual Relating to Iceland and the Fiske Icelandic Collection in Cornell University Library*. Volume IX. Ithaca, New York: Issued by Cornell University Library, 1916.) Pp. (6), xii, 72; 5 plates, illus.

Reviewed in: *The International* (New York) X (1916), 383–84, by Jacob W. Hartmann.
Lögrjetta, 13 Dec. 1916, by Sigfús Blöndal.
Nordisk Tidskrift för Bok- och Biblioteksväsen III (1916), 331–33, by Sigfús Blöndal.
Eimreiðin XXIII (1917), 186, by Valtýr Guðmundsson.
Mitteilungen der Islandfreunde V (1917/18), 20, by Heinrich Erkes.
Skírnir XCI (1917), 199–213, by Páll Eggert Ólason.

Review:

Jón Magnússon, *Píslarsaga. Lögberg*, 6 July 1916.

1917

Articles:

"Enn um skjaldarmerkið." *Eimreiðin* XXIII (1917), 109–11.

"Ole Worm." *Ársrit hins íslenska Fræðafjelags í Kaupmannahöfn* II (1917), 42–64.

Book:

Annalium in Islandia farrago and De mirabilibus Islandiae. By Gísli Oddson, Bishop of Skálholt. Edited with an Introduction and Notes by Halldór Hermannsson. Ithaca, New York: Cornell University Library, 1917. (*Islandica: An Annual Relating to Iceland and the Fiske Icelandic Collection in Cornell University Library.* Volume X. Ithaca, New York: Cornell University Library.) Pp. (6), xv, (1) 84.

Reviewed in: *Cornell Alumni News* XX (1917/18), 171. *Skírnir* XCII (1918), 382–83, by Páll Eggert Ólason.

1918

Articles:

"Jólatrú og jólasiðir." *Lögberg*, 19 Dec. 1918.

"Two letters from Jacob and Wilhelm Grimm." *Journal of English and Germanic Philology* XVII (1918), 79–81.

"Willard Fiske and Icelandic Bibliography." Bibliographical Society of America. *Papers* XII (1918), 97–106.

Books:

Catalogue of Runic Literature Forming a Part of the Icelandic Collection Bequeathed by Willard Fiske. Compiled by Halldór Hermannsson. London. Edinburgh. Glasgow. New York. Toronto. Melbourne. Bombay: Humphrey Milford, Oxford University Press, 1918. Pp. viii, (2), 106; 1 plate. [At head of title: Cornell University Library.]

Reviewed in: *American Historical Review* XXIII (1917/18), 940–41.
Cornell Alumni News XX (1917/18), 403, by [Clark S. Northup].
Lögberg, 18 April 1918, by [J. J. Bildfell].
Skírnir XL (1918), 383, by Páll Eggert Ólason.
Arkiv för nordisk filologi XXXVI (1919/20), 93–94, by Erik Brate.
Deutsche Literaturzeitung XLI (1920), cols. 437–38, by Gustav Neckel.
Anzeiger für deutsches Altertum XL (1920/21), 101–3, by Fritz Burg.
Mitteilungen der Islandfreunde VIII (1920/21), 19, by W. Heydenreich.
Literaturblatt für germanische und romanische Philologie XLIII (1922), col. 370, by Helmut de Boor.

The Periodical Literature of Iceland down to the Year 1874: An Historical Sketch. With thirteen facsimiles and seven portraits. Ithaca, New York: Cornell University Library, 1918. (*Islandica: An Annual Relating to Iceland and the Fiske Icelandic Collection in Cornell University Library*. Volume XI. Ithaca, New York: Issued by Cornell University Library.) Pp. (8), 100; 7 plates, facsims.

Reviewed in: *Eimreiðin* XXV (1919), 253–54, by Magnús Jónsson.
Lögberg, 17 April 1919. [Under heading "Nýútkomin bók."]
Lögrjetta, 10 Sept. 1919, by Matthías Jochumsson.
Cornell Alumni News XXII (1919/20), 434, by [Clark S. Northup].
Iðunn V (1919/20), 154, by Ágúst H. Bjarnason.
Skírnir XCIV (1920), 157–60, by Páll Eggert Ólason.
Nordisk Tidskrift för Bok- och Biblioteksväsen X (1923), 49, by Sigfús Blöndal.

1919

Articles:

"Sir George Webbe Dasent." *Skírnir* XCIII (1919), 117–40.

"Vínlandsferðirnar." *Tímarit Þjóðræknisfélags Íslendinga* I (1919), 25–52.

Book:

Modern Icelandic: An Essay. Ithaca, New York: Cornell University Library, 1919. (*Islandica: An Annual Relating to Iceland and the Fiske Icelandic Collection in Cornell University Library.* Volume XII. Ithaca, New York: Issued by Cornell University Library. Copenhagen: Andr. Fred. Höst & Sön. Reykjavik: Bókaverzlun Sigfúsar Eymundssonar.) Pp. (6), 66.

Reviewed in: *Cornell Alumni News* XXII (1919/20), 434, by [Clark S. Northup].

Lögberg, 1 April 1920.

Iðunn VI (1920/21), 323–34, by Ágúst H. Bjarnason.

Mitteilungen der Islandfreunde VIII (1920/21), 19, by W. Heydenreich.

Deutsche Literaturzeitung XLII (1921), cols. 237–38, by Gustav Neckel.

Eimreiðin XXVII (1921), 118, by Magnús Jónsson.

Anzeiger für deutsches Altertum XLI (1921/22), 75–76, by W. H. Vogt.

Literaturblatt für germanische und romanische Philologie XLIV (1923), cols. 14–15, by F. R. Schröder.

Nordisk Tidskrift för Bok- och Biblioteksväsen X (1923), 48, by Sigfús Blöndal.

Archiv für das Studium der neueren Sprachen und Literaturen CLXIII (1933), 106–7, by H. K. Mueller.

1920

Articles:

"Barbarskir víkingar." *Ársrit hins íslenska Fræðafjelags í Kaupmannahöfn* V (1920), 57–79.

"Endnu en Gang Vinlands Beliggenhed." *Det nye Nord* II (1920), 193–95.

"Landafundir og Sjóferðir í Norðurhöfum." *Tímarit Þjóðræknisfélags Íslendinga* II (1920), 3–16.

"Minni Íslands." *Heimskringla*, 11 Aug. 1920; *Lögberg*, 12 Aug. 1920. Reprinted in *Lögrjetta* XV, 15 Sept. 1920. [Address given in Winnipeg, 2 Aug. 1920.]

"Viðurnefnið 'barnakarl.'" *Árbók hins íslenzka Fornleifafélags* (1920), 3–7.
"Vinlands Beliggenhed." *Det nye Nord* II (1920), 76–77.

Book:

Bibliography of the Eddas. Ithaca, New York: Cornell University Library, 1920. (*Islandica: An Annual Relating to Iceland and the Fiske Icelandic Collection in Cornell University Library.* Volume XIII. Ithaca, New York: Issued by Cornell University Library. Copenhagen: Andr. Fred. Höst & Sön. Reykjavik: Bókaverzlun Sigfúsar Eymundssonar.) Pp. (10), 95.

Reviewed in: *American-Scandinavian Review* IX (1921), 146.
Cornell Alumni News XXIII (1921), 250, by [Clark S. Northup].
Eimreiðin XXVII (1921), 118, by Magnús Jónsson.
Heimskringla, 12 Jan. 1921.
Lögberg, 20 Jan. 1921. [Editorial.]
Lögrjetta, 27 April 1921, by Vilhjálmur Þ. Gíslason.
Journal of English and Germanic Philology XXI (1922), 183–84, by George T. Flom.
Nordisk Tidskrift för Bok- och Biblioteksväsen X (1923), 48–50, by Sigfús Blöndal.

Review:

H. P. Steensby, *The Norsemen's Route from Greenland to Wineland*; Andrew Fossum, *The Norse Discovery of America. American Historical Review* XXV (1919/20), 290–93.

1921

Articles:

"Dante." *Lögberg*, 22 Dec. 1921.
"Enn um Grœnlandsmálið." *Lögberg*, 29 Dec. 1921. [Reply to Einar Benediktsson.]
"Hið íslenzka fræðafélag í Kaupmannahöfn." *Lögberg*, 6 Jan. 1921.
"Ísland og Grænland." *Lögberg*, 24 Nov. 1921. Danish translation in *Berlingske Tidende* (Copenhagen), 19 Feb. 1922.

"Ísland og útlendingar." *Morgunblaðið*, 27 July 1921.
Contribution to "Nordisk bibliografisk litteratur under år 1919," ed. J. L. Samzelius. *Nordisk Tidskrift för Bok- och Biblioteksväsen* VIII (1921), 245–57.
"Þorfinnur karlsefni. Afhjúpun líkneskisins í Fíladelfíu." *Lögrjetta*, 19 Jan. 1921. [Address given at unveiling of a bust of Þorfinn Karlsefni in Philadelphia.]

1922

Articles:

"Nokkur orð um embættaskipun." *Morgunblaðið*, 10 March 1922; *Lögrjetta*, 11 March 1922.
Contribution to "Nordisk bibliografisk litteratur under åren 1920–21," ed. J. L. Samzelius. *Nordisk Tidskrift för Bok- och Biblioteksväsen* IX (1922), 261–86.
"Obituary: Þorvaldur Thoroddsen." *Geographical Review* XII (1922), 502.

Books:

Islænderne i Amerika. (*Dansk-islandsk Samfunds Smaaskrifter*, 12.) Copenhagen: Andr. Fred. Høst, [1922]. Pp. 43, (1 errata sheet).

Icelandic Books of the Seventeenth Century (1601–1700). Ithaca, New York: Cornell University Library, 1922. (*Islandica: An Annual Relating to Iceland and the Fiske Icelandic Collection in Cornell University Library.* Volume XIV. Ithaca, New York: Issued by Cornell University Library. Copenhagen: Andr. Fred. Höst & Sön. Reykjavik: Bókaverzlun Sigfúsar Eymundssonar.) Pp. (8), xiii, (1), 121; 1 plate facsims.

Reviewed in: *Lögberg*, 2 Nov. 1922.
American Historical Review XXVIII (1922/23), 396.
Cornell Alumni News XXV (1922/23), 133, by [Clark S. Northup.]

Eimreiðin XXIX (1923), 190–91, by Magnús Jónsson.
Nordisk Tidskrift för Bok- och Biblioteksväsen X (1923), 50, by Sigfús Blöndal.
Skírnir XCVII (1923), 204–95, by Páll Eggert Ólason.
Literarisches Zentralblatt LXXV (1924), col. 467, by Paul Herrmann.

Review:
G. M. Gathorne-Hardy, *The Norse Discoverers of America. Isis* IV (1921/22), 505–8.

1923

Articles:
"Íslendingar og Danir." *Lögberg*, 8 Feb. 1923.
["Martin Moeller's *Soliloquia Animae.* (Hólar 1677)."] *Harvard Library Notes*, No. 11 (1923), Pp. 230–31.
Contribution to "Nordisk bibliografisk literatur under år 1922," ed. J. L. Samzelius. *Nordisk Tidskrift för Bok- och Biblioteksväsen* X (1923), 237–50.

Review:
G. M. Gathorne-Hardy, *The Norse Discoverers of America. American-Scandinavian Review* XI (1923), 371–72.

1924

Articles:
"The Fiske Icelandic Collection in Cornell University." *Scandinavia* I, No. 6 (1924), 11–15.
Contribution to "Nordisk bibliografisk litteratur under år 1923," ed. Sven Ågren. *Nordisk Tidskrift för Bok- och Biblioteksväsen* XI (1924), 239–55.
"Vilhjálmur Stefánsson." *Ársrit hins íslenska Fræðafjelags í Kaupmannahöfn* XVIII (1924), 1–41.

Book:

Jón Guðmundsson and His Natural History of Iceland. Ithaca, New York: Cornell University Library, 1924. (*Islandica: An Annual Relating to Iceland and the Fiske Icelandic Collection in Cornell University Library.* Volume XV. Ithaca, New York: Issued by Cornell University Library. Copenhagen: Andr. Fred. Höst & Sön. Reykjavik: Bókaverzlun Sigfúsar Eymundssonar.) Pp. (6), xxviii, 40; 9 plates.

Reviewed in: *American Historical Review* XXX (1925), 432.
Eimreiðin XXXI (1925), 94, by Sveinn Sigurðsson.
Literarisches Zentralblatt LXXVII (1926), cols. 1267–68, by Eugen Mogk.
Journal of English and Germanic Philology XXVII (1928), 111–14, by Lee M. Hollander.

Review:

Knut Gjerset, *History of Iceland. American-Scandinavian Review* XII (1924), 561–62.

1925

Articles:

"Æfisaga Jóns Sigurðssonar." *Morgunblaðið,* 26 Aug. 1925.
"Handritaskrá og bókaskrá." *Lögrjetta,* 11 Feb. 1925.

Book:

Eggert Ólafsson: A Biographical Sketch. Ithaca, New York: Cornell University Library, 1925. (*Islandica: An Annual Relating to Iceland and the Fiske Icelandic Collection in Cornell University Library.* Volume XVI. Ithaca, New York: Issued by Cornell University Library. Copenhagen: Andr. Fred. Höst & Sön. Reykjavik: Bókaverzlun Sigfúsar Eymundssonar.) Pp. (6), 56; 1 plate, facsims.

Reviewed in: *Cornell Alumni News* XXVIII (1925/26), 408.
Eimreiðin XXXII (1926), 286–87, by Sveinn Sigurðsson.

Skírnir CI (1927), 227, by Sigurður Nordal.
Journal of English and Germanic Philology XXVII (1928), 111–14, by Lee M. Hollander.

Reviews:

Sigfús Blöndal, *Islandsk-dansk Ordbog*; Geir T. Zoëga, *Icelandic-English Dictionary*; Valtýr Guðmundsson, *Islandsk Grammatik: Islandsk Nutidssprog*; Jakob Jóh. Smári, *Íslenzk setningafræði*. *Modern Language Notes* XL (1925), 171–74.

Wolfgang Golther, *Ares Isländerbuch*. *Journal of English and Germanic Philology* XXIV (1925), 598–99.

1926

Articles:

"Bókmentafjelagið." *Morgunblaðið*, 19 Dec. 1926. Reprinted in *Ísafold*, 3 Jan. 1927.

"Íslenskar bókmentir og erlendar tungur." *Morgunblaðið*, 24 Dec. 1926.

Contribution to "Nordisk bibliografisk litteratur under år 1924," ed. Sven Ågren. *Nordisk Tidskrift för Bok- och Biblioteksväsen* XIII (1926), 43–61.

Book:

Two Cartographers: Guðbrandur Thorláksson and Thórður Thorláksson. With 11 plates. Ithaca, New York: Cornell University Library, 1926. (*Islandica: An Annual Relating to Iceland and the Fiske Icelandic Collection in Cornell University Library*. Volume XVII. Ithaca, New York: Issued by Cornell University Library. Copenhagen: Andr. Fred. Höst & Sön. Reykjavik: Bókaverzlun Sigfúsar Eymundssonar.) Pp. (10), 44; 11 plates.

Reviewed in: *Lögberg*, 30 Dec. 1926.
Cornell Alumni News XXIX (1926/27), 372.
Anzeiger für deutsches Altertum XLVI (1927), 68–69, by Paul Herrmann.

Journal of English and Germanic Philology XXIX (1930), 308–10, by Richard Beck.

Lesbók Morgunblaðsins, 24 Aug. 1930, pp. 257–58. "Islandica Halldórs Hermannssonar," by Richard Beck.

Nordisk Tidskrift för Bok- och Biblioteksväsen XVIII (1931), 224–27, by Sigfús Blöndal.

Speculum VI (1931), 312–13, by F. Stanton Cawley.

Literaturblatt für germanische und romanische Philologie LIII (1932), cols. 13–16, by Harald Spehr.

Journal of English and Germanic Philology XXXII (1933), 89–90, by Lee M. Hollander.

1930

icles:

nkenni Íslendinga." *Morgunblaðið*, 26 June 1930.

entsmiðja Jóns Mattíassonar." *Almanak fyrir árið 1930* [Almaak Ólafs S. Thorgeirssonar] XXXVI (1929), 21–37, 2 plates.

ðleikhúsið." *Morgunblaðið*, 21 Aug. 1930.

ks edited:

thías Þórðarson, *The Vinland Voyages*. Translated by Thorstina ckson Walters. With an Introduction by Vilhjálmur Stefánsn. (American Geographical Society. *Research Series* No. 18. dited by Halldór Hermannsson.) New York: American Geoaphical Society, 1930. Pp. xv, 76; 12 plates.

iewed in: *Canadian Historical Review* XII (1931), 430, by H. P. Biggar.

ographical Journal LXXVII (1931), 380–81, by G. M. Gathorne-Hardy.

w England Quarterly IV (1931), 578–79, by F. Stanton Cawley.

merican Historical Review XXXVII (1931/32), 345–46, by E. L. Stevenson.

glish Historical Review XLVII (1932), 148–49, by G. M. Gathorne-Hardy.

Eimreiðin XXXIII (1927), 110, by Sveinn Sigurðsson.

Geographical Review XVII (1927), 334–35.

Library Association Record, n.s. V (1927), 193, by E. L.

Lögrjetta, 4 Feb. 1927. "Íslensk kortagerð."

Dr. A. Petermanns Mitteilungen LXXIV (1928), 48, by Heinrich Erkes.

Journal of English and Germanic Philology XXVII (1928), 111–14, by Lee M. Hollander.

(*Dansk*) *Historisk Tidsskrift*, 9th ser. VI (1928–29), 331–32, by Finnur Jónsson.

Literaturblatt für germanische und romanische Philologie LI (1930), cols. 328–29, by Helmut de Boor.

1927

Articles:

"Grænlensku fornminjarnar." *Morgunblaðið*, 27 Jan. 1927.

Contribution to "Nordisk bibliografisk litteratur under åren 1925–26," ed. Sven Ågren. *Nordisk Tidskrift för Bok- och Biblioteksväsen* XIV (1927), 209–34.

"Stutt athugasemd." *Morgunblaðið*, 14 April 1927. [Reply to Einar Benediktsson.]

"The Wineland Voyages: A Few Suggestions." *Geographical Review* XVII (1927), 107–14.

Book:

Catalogue of the Icelandic Collection Bequeathed by Willard Fiske: Additions 1913–1926. Ithaca, N.Y.: Cornell University. London: Humphrey Milford. Oxford University Press, 1927. Pp. vii, (3), 284. [At head of title: Cornell University Library.]

Reviewed in: *Cornell Alumni News* XXIX (1926/27), 372.

Literarisches Zentralblatt LXXIX (1927), col. 1954, by Arthur Luther.

Modern Language Notes XLIII (1928), 350–52, by Lee M. Hollander.

Analecta Bollandiana XLVII (1929), 182–83, by P. Grosjean.

Dr. A. Petermanns Mitteilungen LXXVIII (1932), 263, by K. Kretschmer.

Skírnir CIX (1935), 237–38, by Richard Beck.

The Book of the Icelanders (*Íslendingabók*). By Ari Thorgilsson. Edited and Translated with an Introductory Essay and Notes by Halldór Hermannsson. Ithaca, New York: Cornell University Library. London: Humphrey Milford. Oxford University Press, 1930. (*Islandica: An Annual Relating to Iceland and the Fiske Icelandic Collection in Cornell University Library*. Volume XX. Ithaca, New York: Issued by Cornell University Library. London: Humphrey Milford. Oxford University Press. Copenhagen: Andr. Fred. Höst & Sön. Reykjavik: Bókaverzlun Sigfúsar Eymundssonar.) Pp. vi, (2), 89.

Reviewed in: *Bibliographie géographique* XL (1930), 528.

Deutsche Literaturzeitung LI (1930), cols. 2276–77, by Gustav Neckel.

Eimreiðin XXXVI (1930), 435–37, by Guðmundur Finnbogason.

Lesbók Morgunblaðsins, 24 Aug. 1930, pp. 257–59. "Islandica Halldórs Hermannssonar," by Richard Beck.

Lögrjetta, 27 Aug. 1930. "Íslendingabók."

The Scotsman (Edinburgh), 17 July 1930.

Mitteilungen der Islandfreunde XVIII (1930/31), 28–29, by W. Heydenreich.

Modern Philology XXVIII (1930/31), 499–500, by Chester Nathan Gould.

Cornell Alumni News XXXIII (1930/31), 168, by [Clark S. Northup].

Anzeiger für deutsches Altertum L (1931), 200–201, by Hermann Schneider.

Geographical Review XXI (1931), 155–56, by Nels A. Bengtson.

Journal of English and Germanic Philology XXX (1931), 261–62, by Lee M. Hollander.

Literaturblatt für germanische und romanische Philologie LII (1931), cols. 263–65, by Wolfgang Golther.

Modern Language Notes XLVI (1931), 484–86, by Richard Beck.
Nordisk Tidskrift för Bok- och Biblioteksväsen XVIII (1931), 224–27, by Sigfús Blöndal.
Petermanns Mitteilungen LXXVII (1931), 106–7, by Heinrich Erkes.
Revue critique d'histoire et de littérature, n.s. XCVIII (1931), 143–44, by Fernand Mossé.
Speculum VI (1931), 310–12, by F. Stanton Cawley.
History, n.s. XVII (1932/33), 182–83, by G. M. Gathorne-Hardy.
Neophilologus XIX (1933/34), 150, by A. G. van Hamel.
Heimskringla, 11 June 1941, by K. S.

Review:

"Íslensk kvæði á ensku." Review of Richard Beck, *Icelandic Lyrics. Vísir*, 8 July 1930. Reprinted in English translation in *The Quarterly Journal*, published by The University of North Dakota, XX (1931/32), 264–66.

1931

Articles:

"Gamlar íslenskar bækur." *Lesbók Morgunblaðsins*, 1 Feb. 1931, pp. 27–29.

Contribution to "Nordisk bibliografisk litteratur under åren 1927–1928," ed. Sven Ågren. *Nordisk Tidskrift för Bok- och Biblioteksväsen* XVIII (1931), 57–84.

With Vilhjálmur Stefánsson. "Víkingafélagið enska." *Vísir*, 13 Jan. 1931; *Morgunblaðið*, 13 Jan. 1931.

Book:

The Cartography of Iceland. Ithaca, New York: Cornell University Library. London: Humphrey Milford. Oxford University Press, 1931. (*Islandica: An Annual Relating to Iceland and the Fiske Icelandic Collection in Cornell University Library*. Volume XXI. Ithaca, New

York: Issued by Cornell University Library. London: Humphrey Milford. Oxford University Press. Copenhagen: Andr. Fred. Höst & Sön. Reykjavik: Bókaverzlun Sigfúsar Eymundssonar.) Pp. (10), 81; 27 plates (maps, port.).

Reviewed in: *Cornell Alumni News* XXXIV (1931/32), 296.

Mitteilungen der Islandfreunde XIX (1931/32), 98–99, by Heinrich Erkes.

American-Scandinavian Review XX (1932), 250.

Deutsche Literaturzeitung LIII (1932), cols. 947–51, by Hans Kuhn.

Eimreiðin, XXXVIII (1932), 441, by Sveinn Sigurðsson.

Geographical Review XXII (1932), 490.

Geographische Zeitschrift XXXVIII (1932), 503, by H. Rudolphi.

Journal of English and Germanic Philology XXXI (1932), 603–5, by Stefán Einarsson.

Lögrjetta XXVII (1932), cols. 99–100, by Vilhjálmur Þ. Gíslason.

Revue critique d'histoire et de littérature, n.s. XCIX (1932), 44, by E. Metzger.

Revue germanique XXIII (1932), 256–57, by Fernand Mossé.

Zeitschrift der Gesellschaft für Erdkunde zu Berlin, 1932, pp. 319–20, by W. Iwan.

Scandinavian Studies and Notes XII (1932–33), 74–76, by Richard Beck.

Anzeiger für deutsches Altertum LII (1933), 205–6, by Konstantin Reichardt.

Department of Commerce. Bureau of Foreign and Domestic Commerce. Washington. *Geographic News*, I, No. 23 (April 1933), 7.

Geography XVIII (1933), 75, by Arthur Davres.

Isis XIX (1933), 237–40, by Stefán Einarsson.

Lögberg, 9 Feb. 1933, by Richard Beck.

Vísir, 30 July 1934, by Richard Beck.

Nordisk Tidskrift för Bok- och Biblioteksväsen, XXV (1938), 264, by Sigfús Blöndal.

1932

Article:

"Leifur heppni." *Tímarit Þjóðræknisfélags Íslendinga*, XIV (1932), 39–44.

Books:

Codex Frisianus (Sagas of the Kings of Norway): MS. No. 45 Fol. in the Arnamagnaean Collection in the University Library of Copenhagen. With an Introduction by Halldór Hermannsson. (*Corpus codicum Islandicorum medii aevi* IV.) Copenhagen: Levin & Munksgaard, 1932. Pp. (16), (125 unnumbered leaves).

Reviewed in: *Lesbók Morgunblaðsins* VIII (1933), 33–34. "Ejnar Munksgaard og útgáfustarfsemi hans," by Guðmundur Finnbogason.

Skírnir CVII (1933), 227, by Guðmundur Finnbogason.

Sæmund Sigfússon and the Oddaverjar. Ithaca, New York: Cornell University Library. London: Humphrey Milford. Oxford University Press, 1932. (*Islandica: An Annual Relating to Iceland and the Fiske Icelandic Collection in Cornell University Library.* Volume XXII. Ithaca, New York: Issued by Cornell University Library. London: Humphrey Milford. Oxford University Press. Copenhagen: Andr. Fred. Höst & Sön. Reykjavik: Bókaverzlun Sigfúsar Eymundssonar.) Pp. (8), 52; 3 plates.

Reviewed in: *Anzeiger für deutsches Altertum* LII (1933), 205–6, by Konstantin Reichardt.

Eimreiðin XXXIX (1933), 127–28, by Sveinn Sigurðsson.

Journal of English and Germanic Philology XXXII (July 1933), 402–3, by Richard Beck.

Lesbók Morgunblaðsins, 21 May 1933, pp. 145–48.

Lögberg, 9 Feb. 1933, by Richard Beck.

Revue critique d'histoire et de littérature, n.s. C (1933), 261–62, by Fernand Mossé.

Skírnir CVII (1933), 236–38, by Sigurður Nordal.
Modern Philology XXXI (1933/34), 323, by Jan de Vries.
Neophilologus XIX (1933/34), 235–36, by A. G. van Hamel.
Germanic Review IX (1934), 282–83, by Lee M. Hollander.
Vísir, 30 July 1934, by Richard Beck.
Nordisk Tidskrift för Bok- och Biblioteksväsen XXV (1938), 264–65, by Sigfús Blöndal.

1933

Articles:

Contribution to "Nordisk bibliografisk litteratur under åren 1929–1931," ed. Harald J. Heyman. *Nordisk Tidskrift för Bok- och Biblioteksväsen* XX (1933), 1–45.

"The Norsemen's Farthest North in Greenland." *Geographical Review* XXIII (1933), 334–35.

Books:

Old Icelandic Literature: A Bibliographical Essay. Ithaca, New York: Cornell University Press. London: Humphrey Milford. Oxford University Press, 1933. (*Islandica: An Annual Relating to Iceland and the Fiske Icelandic Collection in Cornell University Library*. Volume XXIII. Ithaca, New York: Cornell University Press. London: Humphrey Milford. Oxford University Press. Copenhagen: Andr. Fred. Höst & Sön. Reykjavik: Bókaverzlun Sigfúsar Eymundssonar.) Pp. (6), 50.

Reviewed in: *Archiv für das Studium der neueren Sprachen und Literaturen* CLXIV (1933), 280–81, by Alois Brandl.
La Bibliofilia XXXVI (1934), 329.
Eimreiðin XL (1934), 240, by Sveinn Sigurðsson.
Folk-Lore XLV (1934), 184–85, by Eleanor Hull.
Germanic Review IX (1934), 282–83, by Lee M. Hollander.
Iðunn XVIII (1934), 137–39, by Stefán Einarsson.

Journal of English and Germanic Philology XXXIII (1934), 466–68, by Stefán Einarsson.
Lögberg, 22 Feb. 1934, by Richard Beck.
Skírnir CVIII (1934), 226–27, by Sigurður Nordal.
Times Literary Supplement, 18 Jan. 1934, p. 46.
Vísir, 30 July 1934, by Richard Beck.
Island: Vierteljahrsschrift der Vereinigung der Islandfreunde XX (1934/35), 157, by Alfred Schneider.
Speculum X (1935), 210–11, by Richard Beck.
Nordisk Tidskrift för Bok- och Biblioteksväsen XXV (1938), 265, by Sigfús Blöndal.

Guðspjallabók 1562: Bishop Ólafur Hjaltason's Ritual (*Breiðabólstaður, Jón Matthíasson, 1562*). Facsimile edition with an introduction in English and Icelandic by Halldór Hermannsson. (*Monumenta typographica Islandica*, ed. Sigurður Nordal, vol. II.) Copenhagen: Levin & Munksgaard. Ejnar Munksgaard, 1933. Pp. 47, (1), (48 unnumbered leaves).

Reviewed in: *Nordisk Tidskrift för Bok- och Biblioteksväsen* XXI (1934), 83–84, by Isak Collijn.
Island: Vierteljahrsschrift der Vereinigung der Islandfreunde XX (1934/35), 157, by Alfred Schneider.
Journal of English and Germanic Philology XXXVI (1937), 107–9, by Richard Beck.

Review:

Olaf Klose, *Islandkatalog der Universitätsbibliothek Kiel und der Universitäts- und Stadtbibliothek Köln. Journal of English and Germanic Philology* XXXII (1933), 238–40.

1935

Article:

"Finnur Jónsson." *Journal of English and Germanic Philology* XXXIV (1935), 472–79.

Books:

Icelandic Illuminated Manuscripts of the Middle Ages. (*Corpus codicum Islandicorum medii aevi*, edited by Einar Munksgaard, vol. VII). Copenhagen: Levin & Munksgaard. Einar Munksgaard, 1935. Pp. 32; 80 plates.

Reviewed in: *Skírnir* CIX (1935), 212–13, by Sigurður Nordal.

The Sagas of Icelanders (*Íslendinga sögur*) *: A Supplement to Bibliography of the Icelandic Sagas and Minor Tales.* Ithaca, New York: Cornell University Press. London: Humphrey Milford. Oxford University Press, 1935. (*Islandica: An Annual Relating to Iceland and the Fiske Icelandic Collection in Cornell University Library. Volume XXIV.* Ithaca, New York: Cornell University Press. London: Humphrey Milford. Oxford University Press. Copenhagen: Levin & Munksgaard. Reykjavik: Bókaverzlun Sigfúsar Eymundssonar.) Pp. (2), x, 113.

Reviewed in: *Saga-Book of the Viking Society* XI (1928–36), 299.
Eimreiðin XLI (1935), 361, by Richard Beck.
Island: Vierteljahrsschrift der Vereinigung der Islandfreunde XXI (1935/36), 83, by Reinhard Prinz.
Scandinavian Studies XIV (1936–37), 56–57, by Richard Beck.
Iðunn XIX (1936), 179–80, by Stefán Einarsson.
Revue germanique XXVII (1936), 174, by Fernand Mossé.
Skírnir CX (1936), 218, by Guðmundur Finnbogason.
Archiv für das Studium der neueren Sprachen CLXX (1936), 132, by Annie Heiermeier.
Zentralblatt für Bibliothekswesen LIV (1937), 199–200, by Hildegard Bonde.
Neophilologus XXIII (1937/38), 71, by A. G. van Hamel.
Journal of English and Germanic Philology XXXVII (1938), 320–21, by George T. Flom.
Nordisk Tidskrift för Bok- och Biblioteksväsen XXV (1938), 263, by Sigfús Blöndal.

1936

Article:

Contribution to "Nordisk bibliografisk litteratur under åren 1932–33," ed. Harald J. Heyman. *Nordisk Tidskrift för Bok- och Biblioteksväsen* XXIII (1936), 1–41.

Book:

The Problem of Wineland. Ithaca, New York: Cornell University Press, 1936. (*Islandica: An Annual Relating to Iceland and the Fiske Icelandic Collection in Cornell University Library.* Volume XXV. Ithaca, New York: Cornell University Press. London: Humphrey Milford. Oxford University Press. Copenhagen: Levin & Munksgaard. Reykjavik: Bokaverzlun Sigfusar Eymundssonar.) Pp. (6), 84, (2).

Reviewed in: *American-Scandinavian Review* XXIV (1936), 373.
Iðunn XIX (1936), 361–62, by Stefán Einarsson.
(*Svensk*) *Historisk tidskrift* LVI (1936), 312–13, by Kjell Kumlien.
Scandinavian Studies and Notes XIV (1936–37), 207–8, by Richard Beck.
Anzeiger für deutsches Altertum LVI (1937), 59–60, by Gustav Neckel.
Eimreiðin XLIII (1937), 350–52, by Richard Beck.
English Historical Review LII (1937), 732–33, by A. M.
Geographical Journal XC (1937), 68–69, by M. A. S.
Geographical Review XXVII (1937), 174–75, by Wm. Hovgaard.
Modern Language Notes LII (1937), 463–64, by Stefán Einarsson.
Modern Language Review XXXII (1937), 489, by Angus MacDonald.
New England Quarterly X (1937), 165–67, by Edmund B. Delabarre.
Norsk geografisk tidsskrift VI (1937), 478.
Revue germanique XXVIII (1937), 179–80, by Fernand Mossé.
Skírnir CXI (1937), 216–17, by Ólafur Lárusson.
Times Literary Supplement, 20 March 1937, p. 202.
Neophilologus XXIII (1937/38), 73–74, by A. G. van Hamel.

Deutsche Literaturzeitung LIX (1938), cols. 806–12, by Rudolf Meissner.
Geography XXIII (1938), 67, by J. N. L. Baker.
Literaturblatt für germanische und romanische Philologie LIX (1938), cols. 387–88, by W. H. Vogt.
Nordisk Tidskrift för Bok- och Biblioteksväsen XXV (1938), 265–66, by Sigfús Blöndal.
Petermanns Geographische Mitteilungen LXXXIV (1938), 74, by K. Kretschmer.
Göttingische Gelehrte Anzeigen CCI (1939), 69–88, by Georg Friederici.

1937

Article:
"Sir William Craigie sjötugur." *Skírnir* CXI (1937), 52–55.

Book:
The Sagas of the Kings (*Konunga sögur*) *and the Mythical-Heroic Sagas* (*Fornaldar sögur*)*: Two Bibliographical Supplements*. Ithaca, New York: Cornell University Press, 1937. (*Islandica: An Annual Relating to Iceland and the Fiske Icelandic Collection in Cornell University Library*. Volume XXVI. Ithaca, New York: Cornell University Press. London: Humphrey Milford. Oxford University Press. Copenhagen: Levin & Munksgaard. Reykjavik: Bókaverzlun Sigfúsar Eymundssonar.) Pp. x, 84, (2).

Reviewed in: *Deutsche Literaturzeitung* LIX (1938), col. 812, by Rudolf Meissner.
Eimreiðin XLIV (1938), 349–50, by Sveinn Sigurðsson.
Germanic Review XIII (1938), 306–7, by Lee M. Hollander.
Nordisk Tidskrift för Bok- och Biblioteksväsen XXV (1938), 263–64, by Sigfús Blöndal.
Revue germanique XXIX (1938), 404, by Fernand Mossé.
Skírnir CXII (1938), 208–10, by Stefán Einarsson.

Scandinavian Studies and Notes XV (1938–39), 215–16, by Richard Beck.

Archiv für das Studium der neueren Sprachen und Literaturen CLXXVI (1939), 111–12, by Annie Heiermeier.

Arkiv för nordisk filologi LIV (1939), 379–80, by E. Noreen.

Modern Language Review XXXIV (1939), 483–84, by G. Turville-Petre.

Zentralblatt für Bibliothekswesen LVI (1939), 79, by Hildegard Bonde.

Reviews:

Stefán Einarsson, *Saga Eiríks Magnússonar*. *Modern Language Notes* LII (1937), 134–35.

Marie Simon Thomas, *Onze Ijslandsvaarders in de 17de en 18de eeuw*. *Geographical Review* XXVII (1937), 174.

1938

Book:

The Icelandic Physiologus. Facsimile Edition with an Introduction by Halldór Hermannsson. Ithaca, New York: Cornell University Press, 1938. (*Islandica: An Annual Relating to Iceland and the Fiske Icelandic Collection in Cornell University Library*. Volume XXVII. Ithaca, New York: Cornell University Press. London: Humphrey Milford. Oxford University Press. Copenhagen: Levin & Munksgaard. Reykjavik: Bókaverzlun Sigfúsar Eymundssonar.) Pp. (8), 21, (3); 9 plates.

Reviewed in: *Eimreiðin* XLV (1939), 229–30, by Björn Karel Þórólfsson.

Lögberg, 22 June 1939, by Richard Beck.

Skírnir CXIII (1939), 222, by Jakob Jóh. Smári.

Cornell Alumni News XLII (1939/40), 188, by [Clark S. Northup].

Anzeiger für deutsches Altertum LIX (1940), 28–29, by Helga Reuschel.

Journal of English and Germanic Philology XXXIX (1940), 386–87, by Stefán Einarsson.
Modern Language Notes LV (1940), 541–42, by George T. Flom.
Scandinavian Studies and Notes XVI (1940–41), 318–20, by Richard Beck.
Germanic Review XVI (1941), 156–57, by Lee M. Hollander.
Archiv für das Studium der neueren Sprachen CLXXXI (1942), 53–54, by Annie Heiermeier.
Lychnos, 1946–47, p. 457, by Sten Lindroth.

1939

Articles:

"Fornritaútgáfan—eitt mesta þjóðþrifafyrirtækið." *Lesbók Morgunblaðsins*, 26 March 1939, pp. 89–92.
"Utanríkismál." *Morgunblaðið*, 28 Dec. 1939.

Reviews:

Poul Nörlund, *Viking Settlers in Greenland and Their Descendants during Five Hundred Years*. Translated by W. E. Calvert. *American Historical Review* XLII (1938), 591–93.
Vilhjalmur Stefansson, ed., *The Three Voyages of Martin Frobisher in Search of a Passage to Cathay and India by the North-West, A.D. 1576–78*. *Skírnir* CXII (1938), 225–27.

1940

Articles:

"Íslenskar rímbækur og almanök." In *De libris: Bibliofile Breve til Ejnar Munksgaard paa 50-Aarsdagen 28 Februar*, Copenhagen, 1940, pp. 45–55.
"Vinland." *Encyclopaedia Britannica* (1940). [Reprinted through 1966.]
"The Vinland Voyages." *Le Nord* III (1940) 130–37.

Book:

Illuminated Manuscripts of the Jónsbók. With thirty plates. Ithaca: New York: Cornell University Press, 1940 (*Islandica: An Annual Relating to Iceland and the Fiske Icelandic Collection in Cornell University Library*. Volume XXVIII. *Illuminated MSS of the* Jónsbók . . . Ithaca, New York: Cornell University Press. London: Humphrey Milford. Oxford University Press. Copenhagen: Ejnar Munksgaard. Reykjavik: Bókaverzlun Sigfúsar Eymundssonar.) Pp. (8), 26, (2); 30 plates.

Reviewed in: *Eimreiðin*, XLVI (1940), 387–88, by Stefán Einarsson.

Lesbók Morgunblaðsins, 31 Dec. 1940, pp. 428–29. "Íslenskur listamaður á 17. öld."

Catholic Historical Review XXVI (1940/41), 521.

Scandinavian Studies and Notes XVI (1940–41), 318–20, by Richard Beck.

Germanic Review XVI (1941), 156–57, by Lee M. Hollander.

Times Literary Supplement, 15 Feb. 1941, p. 83.

Heimskringla, 8 April 1942, by Tryggvi J. Oleson.

Modern Language Review XXXVII (1942), 110, by Edith C. Batho.

Speculum XVII (1942), 136–37, by Stefán Einarsson.

Skírnir CXVII (1943), 193–95, by Guðmundur Finnbogason.

1941

Article:

"Columbus og Cabot." *Tímarit Þjóðræknisfélags Íslendinga* XXIII (1941), 1–13.

1942

Book:

Bibliographical Notes. Ithaca, New York: Cornell University Press, 1942. (*Islandica: An Annual Relating to Iceland and the Fiske Icelandic*

Collection in Cornell University Library. Volume XXIX. Ithaca, New York: Cornell University Press. London: Humphrey Milford. Oxford University Press. Copenhagen: Ejnar Munksgaard. Reykjavik: Bókaverzlun Sigfúsar Eymundssonar.) Pp. (8), 91; illus.

Reviewed in: *Eimreiðin* XLIX (1943), 191–92, by Sveinn Sigurðsson.
Heimskringla, 9 June 1943, by H. E. J. Reprinted in *Alþýðublaðið*, 28 Aug. 1943, as "Islandica Halldórs Hermannssonar."
Lögberg, 13 May 1943.
Scandinavian Studies and Notes XVII (1942–43), 317–19, by Richard Beck.
Skírnir CXVII (1943), 193–95, by Guðmundur Finnbogason.
Times Literary Supplement, 23 Oct. 1943, p. 516.
Modern Language Notes LIX (1944), 430–31, by Lee M. Hollander.

1943

Article:
"Goðorð í Rangárþingi." *Skírnir* CXVII (1943), 21–31.

Book:
Catalogue of the Icelandic Collection Bequeathed by Willard Fiske: Additions 1927–42. Compiled by Halldór Hermannsson. Ithaca, N.Y.: Cornell University Press. London: Humphrey Milford. Oxford University Press. Copenhagen: Einar Munksgaard. Reykjavik: Bókaverzlun Sigfúsar Eymundssonar, 1943. Pp. vii, (3), 295. [At head of title: Cornell University Library.]

Reviewed in: *Alþýðublaðið*, 7 July 1943. "Bókaskrá Halldórs Hermannssonar," by Snæbjörn Jónsson.
Eimreiðin XLIX (1943), 192, by Sveinn Sigurðsson.
Journal of English and Germanic Philology XLII (1943), 585–86, by Henning Larsen.

Lögberg, 13 May 1943.
Skírnir CXVII (1943), 195–96, by Guðmundur Finnbogason.

1944

Book:

The Vinland Sagas. Edited with an Introduction, Variants and Notes by Halldór Hermannsson. Ithaca, New York: Cornell University Press, 1944. (*Islandica: An Annual Relating to Iceland and the Fiske Icelandic Collection in Cornell University Library.* Volume XXX. Ithaca, New York: Cornell University Press. London: Humphrey Milford. Oxford University Press. Copenhagen: Ejnar Munksgaard. Reykjavik: Bókaverzlun Sigfúsar Eymundssonar.) Pp. (8), xiv, 75, (3).

Reviewed in: *Alþýðublaðið*, 16 Feb. 1945, by Snæbjörn Jónsson.
Eimreiðin LI (1945), 238, by Geir Jónasson.
Heimskringla, 4 April 1945.
Journal of English and Germanic Philology XLIV (1945), 210–12, by Stefán Einarsson.
Lögberg, 12 April 1945, as "Ný útgáfa af Vínlandssögunum," by Richard Beck.
Skírnir CXIX (1945), 228–30, by Einar Ól. Sveinsson.
Speculum XX (1945), 355–59, by F. P. Magoun.

1945

Book:

The Saga of Thorgils and Haflidi (*Þorgils saga ok Hafliða*). Edited with an Introduction and Notes by Halldór Hermannsson. Ithaca, New York: Cornell University Press, 1945. (*Islandica: An Annual Relating to Iceland and the Fiske Icelandic Collection in Cornell University Library.* Volume XXXI. Ithaca, New York: Cornell University Press. London: Humphrey Milford. Oxford University

Press. Copenhagen: Ejnar Munksgaard. Reykjavik: Bókaverzlun Sigfúsar Eymundssonar.) Pp. (6), 54, (2).

Reviewed in: *American-Scandinavian Review* XXXIV (1946), 186, by Stefán Einarsson.

Eimreiðin LII (1946), 239–40, by Richard Beck.

Germanic Review XXI (1946), 230–31, by Lee M. Hollander.

Scandinavian Studies and Notes XIX (1946–47), 181–82, by Richard Beck.

Skírnir CXXI (1947), 216, by Einar Ól. Sveinsson.

1946

Articles:

"Bókasöfn skólans." In *Minningar úr Menntaskóla*, Reykjavik, 1946, pp. 171–76.

"Fyrstu íslenzku tímaritin." *Helgafell* IV (1946), 209–29. [Translation by Hallgrímur Hallgrímsson of pp. 1–40 of *Islandica* XI.]

1947–48

Articles:

"Ari Þorgilsson fróði." *Skírnir* CXXII (1948), 5–29.

"Ari Þorgilsson og Landnámabók." *Ársrit Skógræktarfélags Íslands*, 1948, pp. 58–63. [Translation by Björn Sigfússon from introduction to *Islandica* XXX, *The Saga of Thorgils and Haflidi*, 1945.]

"Iceland." *Grolier Encyclopedia*. New York: Grolier Society, 1947–48.

1951

Review:

Edward Reman, *The Norse Discoveries and Explorations in America*, 1949. *Speculum* XXVI (1951), 198–99.

1953

Article:

"Íslenzk frímerki." *Lesbók Morgunblaðsins*, 22 Nov. 1953, pp. 649–98.

Review:

Ursula Brown, ed., *Þorgils saga ok Hafliða*. *Scandinavian Studies* XXV (1953), 110–12.

1954

Articles:

"Bibliotheca Arnamagnæana." *Lesbók Morgunblaðsins*, 1 May 1954, pp. 311–14.

"Tyrkir, Leif Erikson's Foster-Father." *Modern Language Notes* LXIX (1954), 388–93.

"Þormóður Torfason." *Skírnir* CXXVIII (1954), 65–94.

1956

Article:

"Sögulegir staðir." In *Nordæla: Afmæliskveðja til . . . Sigurðar Nordals . . . 14. Sept. 1956*, Reykjavik, 1956, 90–96.

1958

Book:

The Hólar Cato: An Icelandic Schoolbook of the Seventeenth Century. Edited with an Introduction and Two Appendices by Halldór Hermannsson. Ithaca, New York: Cornell University Press, 1958. (*Islandica: An Annual Relating to Iceland and the Fiske Icelandic Collection in Cornell University Library*. Edited by Jóhann S. Hannesson. Volume XXXIX. Ithaca, New York: Cornell University Press. Copenhagen: Ejnar Munksgaard. Reykjavik: Bókaverzlun Sigfúsar Eymundssonar.) Pp. xxxiv, 91, (3); 4 plates.

Reviewed in: *American-Scandinavian Review* XLVII (1959), by H. G. Leach.

Arkiv för nordisk filologi LXXIV (1959), 142–43, by K. G. Ljunggren.

Etudes germaniques XIV (1959), 259.

Journal of English and Germanic Philology LVIII (1959), 718–19, by Archer Taylor.

Nationen (Oslo), 3 June 1959, by Helge Refsum.

Scandinavian Studies XXXI (1959) 137–39, by P. M. Mitchell.

Index

Publications Relating to the Fiske Icelandic Collection in the Cornell University Libraries

ISLANDICA

I. *Bibliography of the Icelandic Sagas and Minor Tales.* By Halldór Hermannsson. 1908.*

II. *The Northmen in America (982–c. 1500).* By Halldór Hermannsson. 1909.

III. *Bibliography of the Sagas of the Kings of Norway and Related Sagas and Tales.* By Halldór Hermannsson. 1910.

IV. *The Ancient Laws of Norway and Iceland.* By Halldór Hermannsson. 1911.

V. *Bibliography of the Mythical-Heroic Sagas.* By Halldór Hermannsson. 1912.

VI. *Icelandic Authors of To-day* (with an appendix giving a list of works dealing with Modern Icelandic Literature). By Halldór Hermannsson. 1913.

VII. *The Story of Griselda in Iceland.* Ed. by Halldór Hermannsson. 1914.

VIII. *An Icelandic Satire (Lof Lýginnar).* By Þorleifur Halldórsson, ed. by Halldór Hermannsson. 1915

IX. *Icelandic Books of the Sixteenth Century.* By Halldór Hermannsson. 1916.

X. *Annalium in Islandia farrago and De mirabilibus Islandiæ.* By Bishop Gísli Oddsson, ed. by Halldór Hermannsson. 1917.

XI. *The Periodical Literature of Iceland Down to the Year 1874: An Historical Sketch.* By Halldór Hermannsson. 1918.

XII. *Modern Icelandic: An Essay.* By Halldór Hermannsson. 1919.

XIII. *Bibliography of the Eddas.* By Halldór Hermannsson. 1920.

XIV. *Icelandic Books of the Seventeenth Century.* By Halldór Hermannsson. 1922.

XV. *Jón Guðmundsson and His Natural History of Iceland.* By Halldór Hermannsson. 1924.

XVI. *Eggert Ólafsson: A Biographical Sketch.* By Halldór Hermannsson. 1925.

* Volumes I–XXII were first published by the Cornell University Library; later volumes were published by Cornell University Press. Volumes I–XXXVI have been reprinted by Kraus Reprint Co.

XVII. *Two Cartographers: Guðbrandur Thorláksson and Thórður Thorláksson.* By Halldór Hermannsson. 1926.

XVIII. *Sir Joseph Banks and Iceland.* By Halldór Hermannsson. 1928.

XIX. *Icelandic Manuscripts.* By Halldór Hermannsson. 1929.

XX. *The Book of the Icelanders (Íslendingabók).* By Ari Thorgilsson. Ed. and tr. with an introductory essay and notes by Halldór Hermannsson. 1930.

XXI. *The Cartography of Iceland.* By Halldór Hermannsson. 1931.

XXII. *Sæmund Sigfússon and the Oddaverjar.* By Halldór Hermannsson. 1932.

XXIII. *Old Icelandic Literature: A Bibliographical Essay.* By Halldór Hermannsson. 1933.

XXIV. *The Sagas of Icelanders (Íslendinga sögur): A Supplement to Bibliography of the Icelandic Sagas and Minor Tales.* By Halldór Hermannsson. 1935.

XXV. *The Problem of Wineland.* By Halldór Hermannsson. 1936.

XXVI. *The Sagas of the Kings and the Mythical-heroic Sagas: Two Bibliographical Supplements.* By Halldór Hermannsson. 1937.

XXVII. *The Icelandic Physiologus.* Facsimile edition with an introduction by Halldór Hermannsson. 1938.

XXVIII. *Illuminated Manuscripts of the Jónsbók.* By Halldór Hermannsson. 1940.

XXIX. *Bibliographical Notes.* By Halldór Hermannsson. 1942.

XXX. *The Vinland Sagas.* Ed. with an introduction, variants, and notes by Halldór Hermannsson. 1944.

XXXI. *The Saga of Thorgils and Haflidi.* Ed. with an introduction and notes by Halldór Hermannsson. 1945.

XXXII and XXXIII. *History of Icelandic Prose Writers: 1800–1940.* By Stefán Einarsson. 1948.

XXXIV. *History of Icelandic Poets: 1800–1940.* By Richard Beck. 1950.

XXXV. *The Saga of Hrafn Sveinbjarnarson: The Life of an Icelandic Physician of the Thirteenth Century.* Tr. with an introduction and notes by Anne Tjomsland. 1951.

XXXVI. *The Age of the Sturlungs: Icelandic Civilization in the Thirteenth Century.* By Einar Ól. Sveinsson. Tr. by Jóhann S. Hannesson. 1953.

XXXVII. *Bibliography of the Eddas: A Supplement to ISLANDICA XIII.* By Jóhann S. Hannesson. 1955. (Out of print.)

XXXVIII. *The Sagas of Icelanders (Íslendinga Sögur): A Supplement to ISLANDICA I and XXIV.* By Jóhann S. Hannesson. 1957.

XXXIX. *The Hólar Cato: An Icelandic Schoolbook of the Seventeenth Century.* Ed. with an introduction and two appendices by Halldór Hermannsson. 1958.

XL. *Bibliography of Modern Icelandic Literature in Translation, Including Works Written by Icelanders in Other Languages.* Compiled by P. M. Mitchell and Kenneth H. Ober. 1975.

XLI. *Halldór Hermannsson.* By P. M. Mitchell. 1978.

CATALOGUES

Catalogue of the Icelandic Collection Bequeathed by Willard Fiske. Compiled by Halldór Hermannsson. 1914.*

——: *Additions 1913–26.* 1927.

——: *Additions 1927–42.* 1943.

Catalogue of Runic Literature Forming a Part of the Icelandic Collection Bequeathed by Willard Fiske. Compiled by Halldór Hermannsson. Oxford: Oxford University Press, 1917. (Out of print.)

* This volume and the additions were reprinted in 1960 by Cornell University Press.

Halldór Hermannsson

Designed by R. E. Rosenbaum.
Composed by Syntax International Pte. Ltd.
in 11 point Monophoto Baskerville 169, 2 points leaded,
with display lines in Monophoto Baskerville.
Printed offset by Vail-Ballou Press, Inc.
on Warren's Number 66 Text, 50 pound basis.
Bound by Vail-Ballou Press in
Joanna book cloth,
with stamping in All Purpose Gold foil.

Library of Congress Cataloging in Publication Data
(For library cataloging purposes only)

Mitchell, Phillip Marshall, 1916–
Halldór Hermannsson.

(Islandica ; 41)
"A bibliography of the writings of Halldór Hermannsson": p.
Includes index.
1. Hermannsson, Halldór, 1878–1958. 2. Literary historians—Biography. 3. Librarians—Biography. 4. Icelandic and Old Norse literature—History and criticism. 5. Cornell University. Libraries. I. Series.
PT7127.H4M5 839′.67′072024 [B] 77-14665
ISBN 0-8014-1085-1